Introduction to Java Through Game Development

Learn Java Programming Skills by Working with Video Games

Victor G. Brusca

Apress®

Introduction to Java Through Game Development: Learn Java Programming Skills by Working with Video Games

Victor G. Brusca
Edison, NJ, USA

ISBN-13 (pbk): 978-1-4842-8950-1   ISBN-13 (electronic): 978-1-4842-8951-8
https://doi.org/10.1007/978-1-4842-8951-8

Managing Director, Apress Media LLC: Welmoed Spahr
Acquisitions Editor: Spandana Chatterjee
Development Editor: James Markham
Coordinating Editor: Mark Powers

Cover designed by eStudioCalamar

Cover image by Kate Laine on Unsplash (www.unsplash.com)

Distributed to the book trade worldwide by Apress Media, LLC, 1 New York Plaza, New York, NY 10004, U.S.A. Phone 1-800-SPRINGER, fax (201) 348-4505, e-mail orders-ny@springer-sbm.com, or visit www.springeronline.com. Apress Media, LLC is a California LLC and the sole member (owner) is Springer Science + Business Media Finance Inc (SSBM Finance Inc). SSBM Finance Inc is a **Delaware** corporation.

For information on translations, please e-mail booktranslations@springernature.com; for reprint, paperback, or audio rights, please e-mail bookpermissions@springernature.com.

Apress titles may be purchased in bulk for academic, corporate, or promotional use. eBook versions and licenses are also available for most titles. For more information, reference our Print and eBook Bulk Sales web page at http://www.apress.com/bulk-sales.

Any source code or other supplementary material referenced by the author in this book is available to readers on GitHub (https://github.com/Apress). For more detailed information, please visit http://www.apress.com/source-code.

Printed on acid-free paper

I'd like to dedicate this book to my Mom and Dad and to my Uncle Jimmy and Tianti. I love you all very much.

Table of Contents

About the Author

Victor Brusca is an experienced software developer specializing in building cross-platform applications and APIs. He regards himself as a self-starter with a keen eye for detail, an obsessive protection of systems/data, and a desire to write well-documented, well-encapsulated code. With over 14 years' software development experience, he has been involved in game and game engine projects on J2ME, T-Mobile SideKick, WebOS, Windows Phone, Xbox 360, Android, iOS, and web platforms.

Introduction

In this book, "Learning Java Through Game Development," you will learn the fundamentals of the Java programming language through a detailed review of the language's features, including data structures and OOP, reenforced by coding challenges throughout the text. Get started today by downloading the book's projects and source code here: `http://github.com/apress/introduction-to-java-through-gamedev/` Using the associated game projects along with topic specific coding challenges you will gain experience and knowledge working with the Java programming language, the NetBeans IDE, a 2D game engine, and three different 2D games! This introductory text will give you a solid foundation of experience in Java and video game programming for you to build on.

CHAPTER 1

Introduction

In this book, *Introduction to Java Through Game Development*, you will learn the fundamentals of the Java programming language through hands-on game development tasks. Through the completion of topic-specific coding challenges, focused on a particular aspect of one of the three games included with the text, you will gain experience and knowledge working with the Java programming language, the NetBeans IDE, a 2D game engine, and three different 2D games. And without further ado, allow me to provide some details about this book starting with information on the structure and conventions used in this text.

About This Text

This text will guide you through the basics, and some advanced topics, of the Java programming language. As we proceed through the different topics involved, you will be challenged to alter, fix, write, and/or debug a copy of one of the three games included with the text:

- Pong Clone

- Memory Match

- Dungeon Trap

Each game is written in a proprietary 2D game engine included with the text. The engine is open source and can be accessed here if you want to take a look at the code involved:

github.com/apress/intro-java-through-game-dev

The source code associated with this game project can be found in the same repo.

© Victor G. Brusca 2023
V. G. Brusca, *Introduction to Java Through Game Development*, https://doi.org/10.1007/978-1-4842-8951-8_1

Each project includes a fully functioning version of the game with full source code as well as coding challenges. As you progress through this text, you will be given challenges that apply certain Java programming language knowledge to the game project at hand. There will be specific copies of the game project preconfigured for the current chapter's challenge.

Generally speaking, this text will not require you to be connected to the Internet for prolonged periods of time outside of downloading a copy of this text and its associated code and programs. You will need only a small amount of computing resources to run the associated software and games. You should have a computer with resources at least equal to the following minimum requirements:

- Dual core CPU

- 4GB of system RAM

- 2GB of storage space

Any relatively modern computer should be able to handle the workload without a sweat. When working with any modern programming language, a decision must be made as to how to code in that language. Oftentimes, you can just use Notepad and a few command-line tools to write and build programs. In our case, however, we would like to use more advanced tools, so we'll require the use of an IDE.

An IDE is an Integrated Development Environment and is a fairly complex program whose job it is to make some of the tasks of the software developer easier so they can take on larger projects and focus on the coding at hand. Games are complex programs that often have a lot of moving parts, literally. As such, we stand to benefit greatly by using an IDE, so we chose the NetBeans IDE for our purposes.

Each example game in this text is written for a simple Java 2D game engine. The experience gained from working through the coding challenges in this text will go a long way to giving the reader a solid foundation to create some of their own 2D games in Java using the included game engine.

Notes on Formatting

Throughout the text there are some consistent formatting patterns I would like to discuss. First off, each chapter follows a similar, general structure, listed as follows:

- Chapter Introduction

  - Topic #1

- Topic #2

- Challenge Description

- Challenge Solution

- Chapter Conclusion

The "Topic" and "Challenge" sections are repeated as necessary to touch upon all the chapter's topics and will sometimes vary slightly in their construction. In general, though, each chapter will have a structure close to that outlined previously. In addition to the text, each chapter will have a namespace entry in the associated game project for each challenge in that chapter.

There will be more on this to come. For now, the main takeaway is that each challenge will have a little sandbox copy of the game for you to work with and a completed example to look at. The structure of the code challenges themselves is present in the chapter outline, but in any case, let's discuss them a little bit before we move on.

- Challenge Description

- Challenge Solution

The general structure of the coding challenges presented in the text is listed previously. The challenge will be presented with a detailed description and a clue, if any is provided. Of course, there will be variations in the sections and section titles. The challenges themselves are designed to apply the knowledge learned in the current programming language topic. Challenges can vary but will always be a small development task using the Java programming language topic at hand.

Following every challenge section will be an explanation of the correct way to solve the challenge including screenshots or other resources to demonstrate the proper functionality. We'll also indicate clearly where to look for the completed challenge's code, so you don't have to worry about not understanding how a problem was solved.

That sums up the general structure of the chapters and challenge sections of the text. The overall cadence of the text starts with the fundamental aspects of the Java programming language and works toward more advanced topics and language features.

Notes on Conventions

There are a few conventions in the text we should also discuss before getting further into the text. First off, we have lists of items:

- Item 1

- Item 2

- Item 3

In most cases, these will be simply shown in-line with the text and not be adorned with any special header or caption text. In rare cases where the list has some kind of special significance, it may appear with its own header and caption similar to the way code and images are shown. Code snippets in the text will be presented with a header and caption in the following format:

Listing 1-1. Code Listing Example – SomeClass.java

```
1 int test = 0;
```

Caption for the example code listing from the SomeClass.java file.

Information about what code the snippet is showing can be found in the header text and/or the caption text or the context associated with the code snippet. Line numbers in code snippets are relative to the starting line of the code and are not absolute. The starting line of code is determined by the context of the text, what example the text is currently working with, and always starts at line 1 unless the code is split across multiple listings. Images are presented in a similar fashion, as shown subsequently.

Image 1-1. *Screenshot – Dungeon Trap Main Menu*

A screenshot of the Dungeon Trap game's main menu.

Lastly, there will be places in the text where a tip or aside is listed. There are two types of side notes in the text: notes about game development and notes about the Java programming language. These entries are formatted as follows:

**Game Development Note: A note about Java game development or game engine use.

**Java Programming Note: A detailed note about Java programming.

This listing type will be used to present extended or advanced information on a topic as it's associated with game development or the Java programming language.

Objectives

There are a few objectives that this book hopes to accomplish. The first is a complete review and demonstration of the Java programming language's base features. The second is an introduction to select advanced features of the Java programming language. Lastly, this text is designed to give you experience working directly with game code using the NetBeans IDE and a set of included video game projects. Let's take a look at these objectives in little more detail.

Java Fundamental Topics

The fundamental Java programming language topics covered in this text are listed as follows with a brief description:

- Overview: Programming Computers: A brief overview of programming computers
- The Java Programming Language: A brief history of the Java programming language
- Overview – Game Programming: A brief overview of game programming
- Basic Data Types: Basic data types in Java
- Advanced Data Types: Advanced, custom data types in Java
- Enumerations: Enumeration data types in Java
- Using Variables: Working with variables
- Numeric Expressions: Working with numeric expressions
- Boolean Expressions: Working with Boolean expressions
- If, Else, Else-If Statements: Flow control, if-else statements
- Switch Statements: Flow control, Switch statements
- Using Arrays: Working with arrays in Java
- Basic For Loop: Working with for loops
- While Loops: Working with while loops
- Importing Classes/Libraries: Working with Java classes and libraries

This text will provide you with a solid foundation of experience working with fundamental aspects of the Java programming language. In the next section, we'll look at the advanced Java programming topics that are addressed in this text.

Java Advanced Topics

This text does address some of the more advanced Java programming topics without getting too deep into very advanced programming. You may find these topics a little bit more challenging as they are inherently more complex. We'll provide you with solid information and challenges to help you grasp the material. The advanced topics that are addressed in this text are as follows:

- Custom Data Types: Working with classes and enumerations

- Try-Catch Statements: Using try-catch statements to control flow

- Data Structures Lists: Simple example of using List data structures

- Data Structures Dictionaries: Simple example of using Dictionary data structures

- Generic vs. Specialized Data Structures: Brief introduction to generic and specialized data structures

- For-Each Loop: Using for-each loops

- Overview – Object Oriented Programming: Brief introduction to OOP design and implementation

- Classes: Brief introduction to classes

- Fields: Using class fields

- Methods: Using class methods

- Constructors: Using class constructors

- Static Members: Working with static class members

- Class Access: Talking points on class member access

- Class Design: Talking points on class design and implementation

- Encapsulation: Examples of encapsulation in a Java game project

- Polymorphism: Examples of using polymorphism in a Java game project

- Inheritance: Brief review of inheritance

- Project Structure: Brief review of project structure

- Debugging: Using debugging to trace program errors and issues.

Java programming advanced topics can often lead to a tremendous amount of material to review and discuss. That is outside the scope of this text, so we'll keep our topic discussions and challenges associated with advanced programming topics brief so that we can cover as many topics and material as possible.

Game Development Topics

Due to the introductory nature of this text, we won't cover game development topics directly, but because each challenge in the text is focused on applying the Java programming language knowledge that you learn to an actual video game, you will gain some knowledge and exposure to the following game development topics:

- Project Structure: Experience working with three different games and their classes, project structure.

- Game Resources: Experience working with game resources.

- Game Engines: A full game engine is included with the text and is used by all the example games.

- Main Game Loop: Experience working with and understanding the importance of the main game loop.

That brings us to the conclusion of this section. We've quickly outlined the different topics that we'll cover in the text both directly via topics and challenges, and indirectly by working with parts of a larger more complex project. In the next section, we'll set up your development environment and get the latest copy of the book's code.

Setting Up Your Environment

In this section, we'll get your development environment up and running so that you can take the included game projects for a little test run and see them in action. This will give you an idea of what the projects are all about. First off, we'll need to get the IDE installed and set up. This text uses the NetBeans IDE for Java project management and development.

First off, we need to install a copy of the Java Development Kit (JDK). You can download versions of the Oracle JDK from the `www.oracle.com/java/technologies/` `downloads/` website. You may need an account to download certain versions of the development kit. If you already have a JDK installed, that's fine; however, you should try installing and working with the version of the JDK that the included games were coded against.

At the time of this writing, Java SE 18 is the latest version of the JDK. The included projects were written against Java SE 11 LTS. I recommend using Java SE 11 LTS when working with the included game projects, but you can try working with whatever Java version you like and fall back to Java SE 11 LTS if you run into any issues. You can find the Java 11 JDK here:

`www.oracle.com/java/technologies/downloads/#java11`

Let's install the JDK first, then the NetBeans IDE. I'm working on a Windows computer, so I downloaded the JDK corresponding with my hardware. Double-click the JDK 11 installer you just downloaded. The process should be very straightforward. If you run into any issues during the installation, use the following URL to troubleshoot the process.

`https://docs.oracle.com/en/java/javase/11/install/installation-jdk-microsoft-windows-platforms.html`

Once the JDK is installed, we're going to move on and setup the NetBeans IDE and the included game project. Navigate your favorite browser to the `https://netbeans.` `apache.org` website and download the latest LTS release. At the time of this writing, the NetBeans IDE download link is on the website's main page. Click it, then locate the latest LTS version of the IDE for your computer's OS. The process is depicted in Images 1-2 to 1-5.

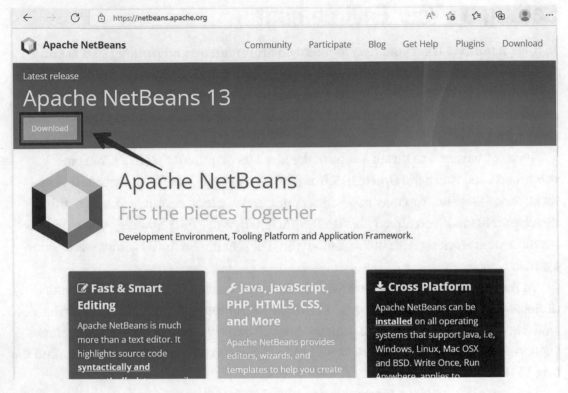

Image 1-2. *Screenshot – NetBeans IDE Download 1*

A screenshot depicting the NetBeans IDE download link at the time of this writing.

Locate the installation binary for your OS. I'm using a 64-bit Windows machine, so I'll choose the appropriate installation binary as shown in the subsequent image.

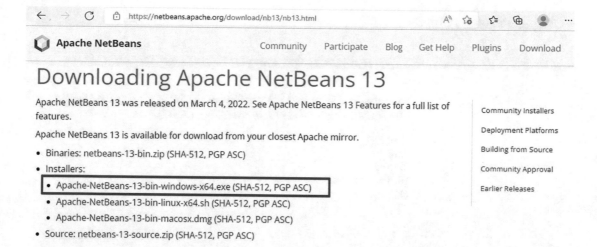

Image 1-3. *Screenshot – NetBeans IDE Download 2*

Make sure to choose the installer that is right for your computer architecture and operating system.

Open the NetBeans IDE installer you downloaded for your target development computer. You should see something similar to that shown in Image 1-4.

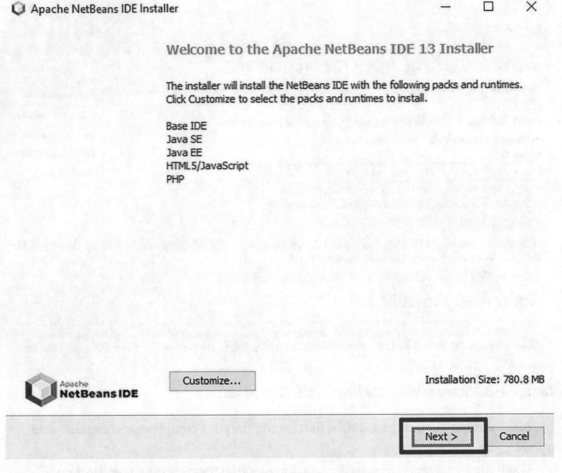

Image 1-4. *Screenshot – NetBeans IDE Installation 1*

Apache NetBeans IDE 13 main installation screen.

We're going to be working exclusively with Java so we can accept the default installation options. Feel free to adjust settings as you see fit, but we recommend just following the default installation options. Before you hit the install button, make sure the "Check for updates" check box is checked (Image 1-5).

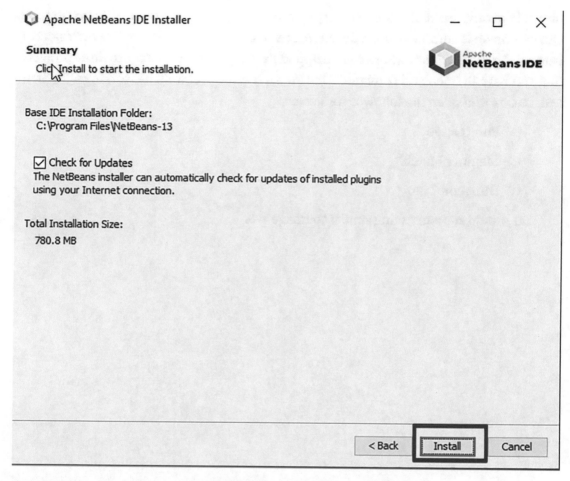

Image 1-5. Screenshot – NetBeans IDE Installation 2

Apache NetBeans IDE 13 installation process, about to install. Make sure to check for updates.

When the installation completes, open up NetBeans and follow any software update prompts. In the next section, we'll install and configure the book's associated game projects.

Getting the Game Projects Setup

Now that you have the JDK and the NetBeans IDE properly installed, you'll need to download a copy of the project associated with this text. You can do so at the following URL: github.com/apress/intro-java-through-game-dev. Download the project ZIP file and decompress it into the directory where you plan to keep your NetBeans projects. Once this step is complete, open the NetBeans IDE and select "File" ➤ "Open Project". Navigate to the directory where you unzipped the project code. There are three projects that you have to open and configure. One for each game that we'll be working with in this text. Locate and open the following projects:

- Pong Clone

- Memory Match

- Dungeon Trap

You should see something similar to Image 1-6.

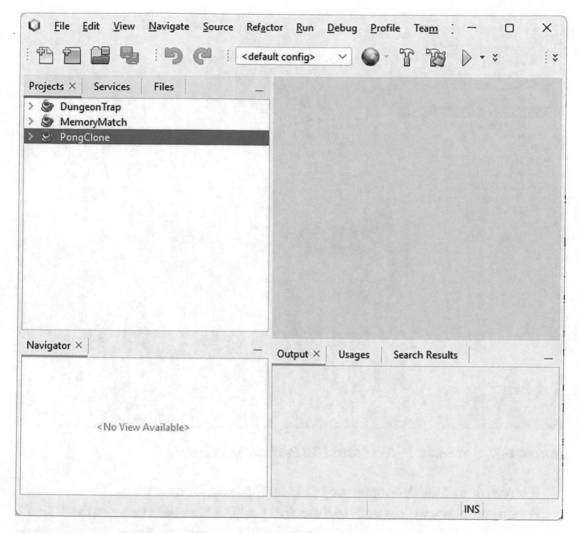

Image 1-6. *Screenshot – NetBeans IDE Opened Projects*

A screenshot of the NetBeans IDE with the game projects opened.

Now that we have the projects loaded, we need to configure them. The first thing we're going to check is that each project has the correct JDK and build directory set. To do so, right-click on each project and select "Properties". We'll check the "Packaging" configuration first. Select the "Build" option's "Packaging" entry on the left-hand side of the properties dialogue (Image 1-7).

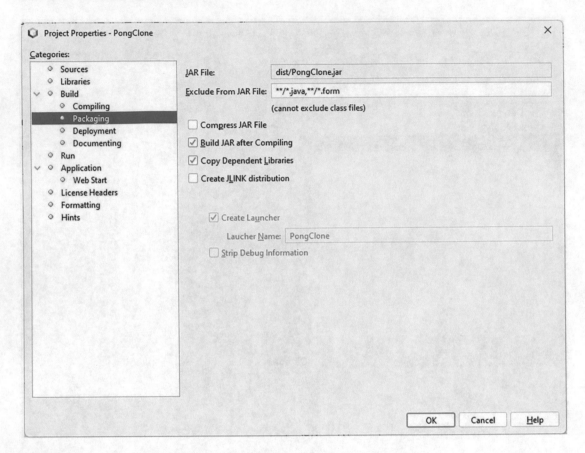

Image 1-7. *Screenshot – NetBeans IDE Packaging Property*

A screenshot of the Packaging properties for the Pong Clone project.

For this property, we just want to check that the "JAR File" path includes the "./dist/" directory. Next, select the "Run" option from the "Categories" list. Remember, we want to check this for each game project (Image 1-8).

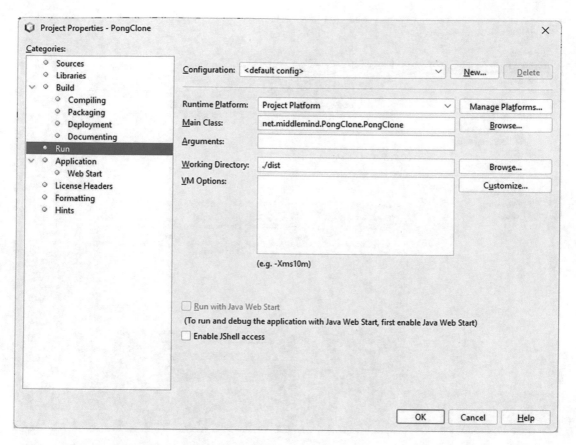

Image 1-8. *Screenshot – NetBeans IDE Run Property*

A screenshot showing the Run property of the Pong Clone project.

For this project property, we want to make sure that the "Working Directory" is set to the directory where the project JAR file will be built. By default, this is the "./dist" directory. Lastly, select the "Sources" entry in the "Categories" list (Image 1-9).

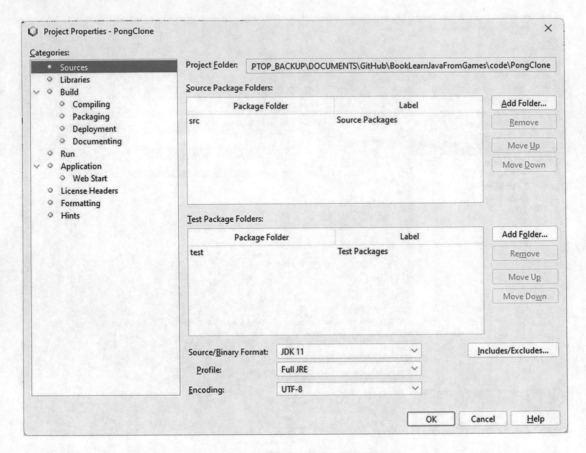

Image 1-9. *Screenshot – NetBeans IDE Sources Property*

A screenshot showing the Sources project settings with JDK 11 selected.

The "Sources/Binary Format" field should be set to "JDK 11". If you were planning to try running the games against a different JDK, this is where you would change the project settings. Again, make sure you perform these project settings checks for each game project. The last thing we need to do before we can play the games is make sure the project libraries are properly mapped. To do so, select the "Libraries" option in the "Categories" list of the project properties dialogue (Image 1-10).

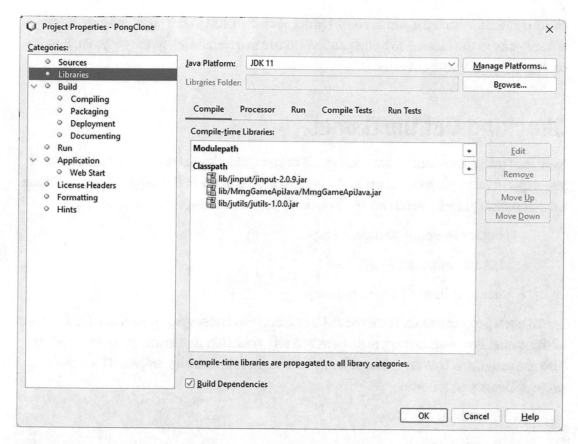

Image 1-10. *Screenshot – NetBeans IDE Libraries Property*

A screenshot showing the libraries category of the project settings with three libraries properly configured.

Each game project should have the same three libraries configured. I'll list them here:

- jinput: ./lib/jinput/jinput-2.0.9.jar

- jutils: ./lib/jutils/jutils-1.0.0.jar

- MmgGamcApiJava: ./lib/MmgGameApiJava.jar

To add a library, select the "+" button adjacent to the "Classpath" label and locate the JAR file listed previously. Each game has its own local "lib" folder with a copy of the required JAR files. Once the libraries are properly mapped, we can move on to the fun part and test the different games. Close the project properties dialogue if it's still opened and right-click the first game project, Dungeon Trap; select "Clean and Build" from the context menu. Watch the project build process and ensure that it completes without error. Perform the clean and build process on the two remaining game projects. Ensure each can be built without error.

Checking Out the Games

Now let's take a moment to run each game project and play around with it a little bit. If you expand each project and expand the source code entry in the project tree, you'll see a main namespace for each project. The main project namespaces are as follows:

- net.middlemind.DungeonTrap

- net.middlemind.PongClone

- net.middlemind.MemoryMatch

In each project's main namespace lies all the Java classes that power the final version of the game. For each namespace, there will be a main file that is the static entry point into the program. This Java class will have the same name as the project. The main project files are as follows:

- DungeonTrap.java

- PongClone.java

- MemoryMatch.java

You'll notice a number of namespaces with names like "PongClone_Chapter1_Challenge1". These are the sandbox environments for handling the different challenges throughout the text. We can ignore those namespaces for now. For each game project, right-click the main file and select the "Run" option. You should see the main menus corresponding with each game (Image 1-11).

Image 1-11. *Screenshot – NetBeans IDE Game Demos*

Image 1-11. (*continued*)

Image 1-11. (*continued*)

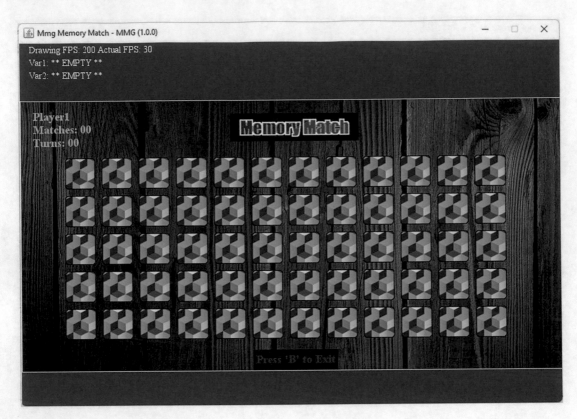

Image 1-11. (*continued*)

Image 1-11. (*continued*)

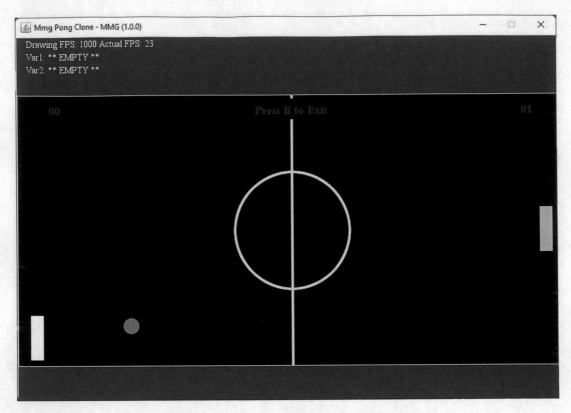

Image 1-11. (*continued*)

A series of screenshots depicting the main menu of each sample game included with the text.

That wraps up the game demonstration section. I hope you enjoyed the little games and are excited to start learning the Java programming language and trying some coding challenges!

Conclusion

To conclude this introductory chapter, I'd like to point out that what we just did was pretty remarkable. We went from 0 to 60 in just a few seconds. Installing the JDK, installing the IDE, followed by downloading, configuring, and running three game projects. That is an example of the power of Java. You'll be sure to see more examples as you take on different coding challenges designed to apply your Java programming language knowledge. Let's take a moment to review the chapter's material.

What We Covered

In this brief introductory chapter, we managed to cover quite a lot of ground:

- Basic Java Topics Covered: We listed and described the basic topics we'll cover throughout the text.

- Advanced Java Topics Covered: We also listed and described the advanced topics we'll cover in this text.

- The JDK: We learned about the Java Development Kit and the target JDK 11 LTS that's used by the book's associated game projects. We also learned that the NetBeans IDE may use its own JRE that's different than the one included in JDK 11.

- The IDE: We learned about the NetBeans IDE, downloaded and installed it.

- Configuring the Game Projects: We took a deep dive into the world of Java game development and prepared three game projects for use in our development environment.

- Games, Games, Games: We got to build and demo three game projects of varying complexity as an introduction to the games we're going to be working with throughout this text.

That brings us to the end of the introduction chapter. In the next chapter we'll start our Java programming education with an overview of what it means to "program" a computer followed by a brief history of the Java programming language and a few other interesting topics.

CHAPTER 2

What Is Java Programming

If you've decided to start learning how to program in Java and you've read this far, it's probably a good idea to talk about what Java programming actually is. In this chapter, we'll take a brief stroll down memory lane and talk, at a high level, about programming computers and what it means to program in Java. We'll also talk about game programming and discuss the venerable main game loop.

Before we get into the origin story behind the Java programming language, let's take a moment to talk about programming computers in general. In the next few sections, we'll explore programming computers using different tools and work our way up to the modern, IDE-based approach. Let's have a look.

Computers and Programming

In this section, we're going to discuss what programming a computer actually means. If you search the phrase online, you might find a definition similar to the following:

"Computer programming is the process that professionals use to write code that instructs how a computer, application, or software program performs[1]. At its most basic, computer programming is a set of instructions to facilitate specific actions."

Although it is fairly accurate, I have one issue with this statement. The use of the word "professionals." One doesn't need to be a "professional" to program computers; anyone can do it! Let's explore this idea a little further and discuss some different ways one can program a computer.

---

[1] https://www.snhu.edu/about-us/newsroom/stem/what-is-computer-programming#:~:text=Computer%20programming%20is%20the%20process,instructions%20to%20facilitate%20specific%20actions.

© Victor G. Brusca 2023
V. G. Brusca, *Introduction to Java Through Game Development*, https://doi.org/10.1007/978-1-4842-8951-8_2

Programming Computers

Programming computers can take on a few different forms. I want to focus on a specific aspect of computer programming and use it to illustrate the importance of Java. We stated previously that a program was a "set of instructions to facilitate specific actions" on a computer. Cleverly hidden in this statement is the concept of a programming language.

The "set of instructions" referenced in the definition is the programming language the software developer is using to write the specific "set of instructions" to solve the given problem with a computer program. One such fundamental set of instructions is the CPU's assembly instruction set. At one point in time, software was written using these archaic tools. An example of assembly programming is shown in Listing 2-1.

Listing 2-1. Assembly Source Code Example

```
1 label_                 ;branch label
2 LSL      R0, R1, #0     ;5.1
3 LSL      R0, R1, #31
4 LSR      R0, R1, #0
5 LSR      R0, R1, #31
6 ASR      R0, R1, #0
```

An example snippet of assembly source code.

The example snippet of assembly source code shows a piece of a larger program. Programming in this medium has its benefits, but it also has its drawbacks. One such drawback is the time it takes to write a program using pure assembly. Assembly source code isn't very intuitive, and this leads to difficulties when programming with it. The language is not very expressive, as you can see. There is little in the way of contextual meaning that can be derived from the lines of assembly in Listing 2-1. This makes it difficult to write complex, abstract, or complicated software using assembly programming.

Programming Languages

In order to address the shortcomings of assembly programming software, developers began creating programming languages. These "languages" were text-based encodings that could be converted into assembly source code and, subsequently, associated binary code.

The benefit of this approach is that the software generated with higher-level languages was easier to read and understand. Writing programs became more expressive, and complex programs became easier to manage than with assembly alone. An example of a higher-level language, C, is shown in Listing 2-2.

Listing 2-2. C Programming Language Example

```
1 #include <stdio.h>
2 int main()
3 {
4     printf("Hello World");
5     return 0;
6 }
```

An example C program.

Higher-level programming languages offered increased capabilities in code reuse, code sharing, and project management. At this point in the history of computers, circa 1983, the C++ programming language became the de facto "set of instructions" used to program computers. While this language provided great power in its object-oriented software design support, it also created a fairly pervasive and troublesome issue.

One core issue that caused many C++ developers hours and hours of debugging time is the concept of memory leaks. Listing 2-3 depicts a very simple C++ program that creates a memory leak.

Listing 2-3. C++ Programming Language Memory Leak Example[2]

```
1 int main() {
2     //safe use of memory
3     int * p = new int;
4     delete p;

5     //unsafe use of memory
6     int * q = new int;
7     //no delete, memory leaked
8 }
```

---

[2]https://stackoverflow.com/questions/7242493/how-to-create-a-memory-leak-in-c

A snippet of source code from a C++ program showing a memory leak.

This simple example program demonstrates how easy it is to leak memory in C++, and memory leaks can cause all types of issues. This is where Java comes to the rescue. One of the main features of the Java programming language is that it has a built-in garbage collector that takes care of deleting unused objects, freeing up memory, preventing any costly memory leaks, and saving tons of debugging time.

We'll spend a little bit more time talking about Java technology and the history of the language, but for now, I'd like to switch directions just a bit and talk about some of the different types of programs software developers write and where Java fits in.

Types of Programs/Programming

There are a lot of different computer programs you can write. Some are very low level and are written in assembly or a system programming language like C, Rust, or Go. Some are higher-level programming languages that support object-oriented programming (OOP) design like C++, Java, or Python.

Furthermore, there are languages designed for very specific programs like JavaScript for web programming, or R for programming statistical computations. Different programming languages have different attributes about them, just like any tool. Some languages are compiled, while some are interpreted. A compiled language usually results in an executable file that contains a binary representation of the original program.

Other languages are interpreted programming languages. An interpreted programming language is compiled but not into machine code. Instead, an interpreted programming language is compiled into an intermediary form that is understood by the programming language's interpreter. The interpreter is a special program that will run the intermediary code and subsequently execute the program.

There are a lot of important aspects of a programming language, but we'll only touch upon the most important ones. The main attributes of the Java programming language are that it's a strongly typed, interpreted programming language with OOP support. We'll cover what it means for Java to be strongly typed when we cover variables in Java. For now, it's enough to understand what this means in a simple way.

Java keeps track of and cares about the data type of any given variable in a program and doesn't let you store data in a variable that is of a different type. Some languages, like JavaScript, have dynamic typing. This means that in JavaScript, you can store any data type in any variable you want without doing a redeclaration. There will be more on this to come during the programming language review.

Just like any tool, different programming languages have different best uses. The Java programming language is good for a number of different things, from applications to web servers and even games. Now, to be fair, Java isn't usually the first go-to language for building games. This is generally because the interpreted nature of the language takes up some small overhead that game developers do not like. The vast majority of games won't miss this small overhead and would probably benefit from the order and simplicity that using Java provides.

However, it remains that Java is a solid programming language and its interpreted nature and inherent support for garbage collection make it a great choice for learning how to program and in particular learning how to program games. The design of a video game is different than that of most other programs. Game programming requires you to build a program that responds in real time to user input while at the same time handling all of the game's video, audio, collision detection, enemy AI, etc., to maintain the illusion of the game. All the while doing so without losing any frames and keeping a smooth animation.

Game programming stands apart from other types of software development due to the specific and sometimes extreme requirements that games have. All that being said, Java is a great language to learn and a great language to learn by working on video games! That brings us to the end of this section. In the next section, we'll take a quick stroll down memory lane and talk a bit about the history of the Java programming language.

The Java Programming Language

Java was born at Sun Microsystems in 1991 when a team of Sun engineers, James Gosling, Mike Sheridan, and Patrick Naughton, sought to create a new programming language that was independent of the processor and could easily run on smaller electronic devices. This is an important oversight of the history of Java and perhaps the reason why Java became a fundamental part of the Android project.

The team created a programming language with a similar C++ like syntax that could run on a small digital remote and control electronic elements like buttons and screens. The project, the "Green Project" meant to explore the convergence between digitally controlled home electronic devices and computers, ultimately failed, but before the Java language was forever lost to time, there was a potentially new application for it, the World Wide Web.

In 1993, the HTTP protocol and one of the first browsers, Mosaic, arrived on the technology scene. During this time, the Java team realized that the Internet would be perfect for the hardware-agnostic attributes of the Java programming language, and in 1995, James Gosling unveiled a browser called WebRunner that supported HTML content and embedded Java applets.

That solidified Java's popularity, and as the early Internet took off, so did Java. Long before flash, the only way you could really create an interactive experience online was by using Java applets. In fact, when I first started out in college, Java applets using AWT were one of the first things they taught us in computer science.

Applets are no longer a supported feature of most browsers. But Java has found its way into many other aspects of modern cloud-based technology both on the server side using Java EE/Jakarta and on the client side with Android, which is based on an open source clone of the Java programming language.

The ability of Java to be written once and "run everywhere" seems almost magical. How can Java run on all these different devices and in all the different places that it seems to? The answer is the Java Runtime Environment (JRE) and the Java virtual machine (JVM).

The JRE

The JRE, and more specifically the Java virtual machine, is responsible for actually executing the Java byte code that is the result from compiling Java source code. Remember, Java is an interpreted language, meaning that a compiled Java program is not in a binary form that can be run by the given CPU. Rather, a virtual CPU, a.k.a. virtual machine, runs the byte code and drives the underlying hardware.

A definition for what the JRE is can be found on the Amazon Web Services (AWS) website. It reads as follows:

> The Java Runtime Environment (JRE) is software that Java programs require to run correctly. Java is a computer language that powers many current web and mobile applications. The JRE is the underlying technology that communicates between the Java program and the operating system. It acts as a translator and facilitator, providing all the resources so that once you write Java software, it runs on any operating system, with a JRE, without further modifications.

> —From the Amazon Web Services site

I find this definition to be very concise and accurate. The last sentence is where the magic really happens. Once "you write Java software, it runs on any operating system, with a JRE, without further modifications"; this is extremely powerful and the second major selling point of the Java programming language, in my humble opinion.

Notice that Java not only includes a programming language and libraries, it also includes/requires a runtime environment to execute Java byte code. This is very different from previous development environments using languages like C and C++ where great care had to be taken to make sure that the language, its data types, and core libraries all performed the same on different computer hardware.

Now with the power of the JRE at your fingertips, you can leverage it to run your Java programs on any operating system, including different hardware architectures like ARM, so long as there's a JRE for that OS. In the next section, we'll take a look at the second most important piece of the Java programming language, the JDK.

The JDK

The Java Development Kit (JDK) is a fundamental aspect of developing software with the Java programming language. The JDK is a collection of software tools that you need to develop Java applications. You can download the JDK and start writing Java programs with just a text editor. In fact, we already installed the JDK, Java 11 SE LTS, and an IDE, NetBeans, so we're ready to start coding.

Now that we've covered the main aspects of Java software development in more detail, let's take a very high-level view of the syntax and semantics of Java programming. You can expect to get a fair amount of experience working with syntactically correct Java code through the completion of the challenges throughout the text.

Syntax and Semantics

What is the correct syntax? In the world of software development, syntax is the set of rules that defines the combinations of symbols that are considered to be correctly structured statements or expressions in that language[3]. Sounds simple enough. We deal with syntax a lot in our everyday lives. Language and grammar all have a syntax. This is often the analogy that is used to explain the syntax of programming languages.

---

[3]https://en.wikipedia.org/wiki/Syntax_(programming_languages

Did I use the correct semantics? Well... maybe? Semantics with regard to programming languages becomes a bit of a complicated topic. Let's explore the idea of semantics a little further. If syntax refers to the grammar of a language, then semantics refers to meaning expressed by the syntactically correct statements in that language.

In human languages, this roughly translates to you saying something that makes sense. Of course, you could obey all the rules of grammar and still not say anything coherent or sensical. The same can be said for computer languages. But in this case, the concept of semantics becomes slightly fuzzy as there are certainly many ways to express one solution correctly. Just as there are many ways to convey the same meaning in human languages.

While you will have to learn and master syntax first in your Java programming language development, you can't compile a program with a syntax error. You can, and will, write programs that are semantically incorrect. Over time you will develop the skill necessary to define the problem you are trying to solve in a correctly structured Java program. Think of it as learning the idiomatic expressions of a new human language you have mastered the grammar, syntax, of. It will take you some time to express yourself fluently in that language.

The same applies to programming languages. You have to learn the correct way to structure programs and approach problems, and that's a skill that you'll develop and refine over time. For now, let's take a look at the core syntax rules of the Java programming language.

Basic Syntax Rules

In this section, we'll briefly review the Java programming language's basic syntax rules. We'll focus on the fundamentals of the language. The following points are important to keep in mind when writing Java code[4]:

- Case Sensitivity: Java is case sensitive, which means the identifiers `Hello` and `hello` would have different meanings in a Java program.

- Class Names: For all class names, the first letter should be uppercase. If several words are used to form a name of the class, each inner word's first letter should be uppercase, referred to as upper camel-case, that is, `SomeClassName`.

---

[4]https://www.tutorialspoint.com/java/java_basic_syntax.htm.

- Method Names: All method names should start with a lowercase letter. If several words are used to form the name of the method, then each inner word's first letter should be uppercase, camel-case, that is, `someMethodName`.

- Program File Name: The name of the program file should exactly match the class name. In fact, the Java compiler will complain if there isn't a public class that matches the current Java file's name.

- Classes[5]: Each class should be in a separate file with a .java extension. Class files are usually grouped into folders. These folders are called packages.

- Programs: The beginning of Java program processing always starts in the main method: `public static void main(String[] args)`. A static main method is a required part of any Java program but not necessarily for a Java library.

- Blocks and Statements: In Java syntax, there are delimiters "{...}" that denote a block of code and a new area of code. Each code statement must end with a semicolon.

- Keywords/Reserved Words: These are special words that cannot be used by the software developer to name symbols like classes, methods, variables, etc.

Syntax is something you'll learn with experience. The IDE will go a long way to detecting any syntax errors before you even hit the compile button. One other thing we want to touch upon before we move on is the set of reserved words in the Java programming language. This is listed as the last point in the summarized list of basic syntax rules.

Keywords/Reserved Words

As with any programming language, Java has a set of words used explicitly by Java itself, and as such, you aren't allowed to use them to create symbols, classes, methods, variables, etc., in your programs. The keywords of the Java programming language are shown in Listing 2-4. There are two reserved words that aren't currently in use by Java but are, however, restricted from use in the same way as keywords.

---

[5]`https://codegym.cc/groups/posts/java-syntax`

Listing 2-4. The Java Programming Language Keywords/Reserved Words[6]

abstract	continue	for	new	switch
assert	default	goto*	package	synchronized
boolean	do	if	private	this
break	double	implements	protected	throw
byte	else	import	public	throws
case	enum	instanceof	return	transient
catch	extends	int	short	try
char	final	interface	static	void
class	finally	long	strictfp	volatile
const*	float	native	super	while

Words adorned with an Asterix, *, indicate reserved words.

You aren't expected to memorize these words right now. You'll get to know them as you gain experience with the language. The main takeaway here is that there are reserved words that you can't use, as is, in your program as symbols, classes, methods, variables, etc.

That brings us to the end of this section. Before we wrap up the chapter, I want to talk a little bit about game programming. We'll be working with three different games to learn about Java programming, so we should have a little background on game programming in general as well as the games we'll be working with.

Game Programming

I'd be remiss in my duty if I didn't spend a little bit of time talking about game programming. After all, we will be using three different games in our challenges as we explore the Java programming language. As I mentioned earlier, video games are a rather unique and challenging type of program. They often require real-time response, intelligent computer opponents, complex input, video, music, sound effects, and multiplayer/network support. That requires a video game developer to master the APIs necessary to do just about everything a computer can do.

Fear not, game engines can help take much of that responsibility off of your shoulders. The games that are included in this book actually incorporate a compact 2D game engine. Each game is a self-contained project including a full engine source

---

[6]https://stackoverflow.com/questions/7242493/how-to-create-a-memory-leak-in-c

code all running in a little Java program. You'll gain experience programming games in challenges designed to demonstrate understanding of Java programming language features.

While we won't attempt to build a game from scratch in this introductory text, you will get some solid game programming experience. Furthermore, you'll gain experience working with the Application Programming Interface (API) of a game engine, and you can use this knowledge to write your own games.

An important piece of introductory information, with regard to game programming, is the main game loop. The main game loop is a common attribute of games and game engines alike; it is a special structure that occurs in almost every game. It is fundamental to game programming, and as such, we'll talk about the main game loop in a little bit more detail in the next section. We'll also encounter this topic again, a little later in the text, and in much more detail.

The Main Game Loop

The main game loop is a common structure that occurs in just about every video game around. The code that makes a video game interactive and dynamic runs in the main game loop but is separated into different main responsibilities. The loop itself is a controlled infinite loop that makes a game run in real time; it's the place where all the objects in your game will be updated and subsequently drawn on the screen[7].

The basic responsibilities of a game loop can be broken down into the following steps, initialize, update, and draw. The initialize step can occur at different times in the life cycle of a game, but it must occur at some point. The update step is where all the game logic runs. This is the code where things like collision detection, hits, sound effects, enemy AI, etc., are handled. Lastly, now that the game state has been updated, it's time to draw the new game state on the screen. That's where the draw step comes in. Also keep in mind that depending on the game in question, networking could be added into the update step.

The main game loop will contain a sync with network objects in the case of a networked multiplayer game. That's the structure of the main game loop, and it's something you should keep in mind when working on game programming. In the next section, we'll talk about the general structure of the included game projects. This will give us a hand when we start navigating around the different project's classes.

---

[7]https://gamedevelopment.tutsplus.com/articles/gamedev-glossary-what-is-the-game-loop--gamedev-2469

Program Structure

The three games included with the text (Dungeon Trap, Memory Match, and Pong Clone) all use the same game engine. The Java version of the MmgGameApi 2D game engine. The entire engine exists in the included MmgGameApiJava.jar file. In general, the increasing complexity of the projects is as follows:

- Pong Clone: Easy

- Memory Match: Moderate

- Dungeon Trap: Expert

Each project contains a custom version of the following Java classes along with proprietary supporting classes:

- Static Main Class: Has the same name as the game itself. Each package, including each challenge package, has a static main for executing that version of the game.

- MainFrame.java: The parent of the GamePanel class that represents the main window frame that holds the game panel.

- GamePanel.java: The main class responsible for drawing, processing input, switching screens, and much more.

- ScreenGame.java: The screen class that runs the game.

- ScreenMainMenu.java: The screen class that runs the game's menu screen.

The game classes are a bit complex, so don't try to edit them on your own just yet. By the end of the book, you should be able to work with them just fine, but we have a bit of ground to cover before then. In the subsequent section, we'll describe the games included with the text in a little more detail.

Overview of Included Games

Even though you got a chance to check out the actual games in the first chapter, let's take a look at a brief description of each game.

1. Pong Clone: A simple two-player clone of the "Pong" video game. Players use different controls to move paddles up and down in order to keep a ball in play. The game uses AI enemy logic when playing in single-player mode. This is the simplest of the three games and includes only five Java classes.

2. Memory Match: A simple solitaire-style memory game that also supports two-player mode to share in the memory matching fun. The game supports three modes of increasing difficulty using more memory cards. This is the second most complex game in the set.

3. Dungeon Trap: A unique mini game where players are stuck in a dungeon room that is flooded with waves of enemies. Fight to stay alive and collect different power-ups to stay in the fight. You can even throw the furniture across the room to send enemies flying. This is the most complex of the three games and includes a number of Java classes. Despite the complexity, it follows the same basic structure as the other games, and the extra code logic is mainly used in the Java classes that actually run the game.

That brings us to the conclusion of this section and the end of this chapter. I hope the game descriptions piqued your curiosity just a bit if the actual games did not. Let's wrap up the chapter with a summary of the main topics that we've covered before moving on to our first chapter on the Java programming language.

Conclusion

In this chapter, we took a look at what it means to program computers and more specifically what it means to program using the Java programming language. We got to look at some high-level aspects of the language and focused on some key features of the types of programs we're going to be working with. Let's summarize the material we covered.

What We Covered

A fair number of important, albeit high-level, topics were covered in this chapter, setting up a solid foundation for us to build up our knowledge of Java as we begin to explore the language. A summary of this chapter's main topics follows:

- Programming Computers: We talked briefly about programming computers with special instructions designed to solve certain problems.

- Programming Languages: We introduced the ideas of programming in languages like C and C++ including some of the difficulties created by managing memory in those languages.

- Types of Programs/Programming: A brief discussion about the different types of programs you can create with Java.

- The Java Programming Language: A brief history of the Java programming language.

- The JRE: We talked about the Java Runtime Environment and spoke of the version we installed in Chapter 1.

- The JDK: We talked about the requirements to Java software development and discussed the Java Development Kit.

- Basic Syntax Rules: A listing of some of the Java programming language's base syntax rules.

- Keywords/Reserved Words: A listing of the keywords and reserved words of the Java programming language.

- The Main Game Loop: A discussion about the main programming loop and its responsibilities.

- Program Structure: We reviewed the core, shared, structure of the three included video games.

- Overview of Included Games: We described the different games and categorized them based on complexity.

Now that we've got that foundational material out of the way, we're ready to start working with the Java programming language. In the next chapter, we'll look at variables in Java.

CHAPTER 3

Variables

Our first foray into learning the Java programming language will be the exploration of variables! Variables are vitally important to any program, and indeed, no useful program could exist without relying on them, all sorts of them. Variables represent data and are often used to track a value throughout a program or method. Sometimes, variables are used as an indicator, a flag, to mark when some important data or event has been encountered. There are many different uses for variables in a Java program, and you'll encounter them as you solve different problems with Java.

We'll be reviewing a few different aspects of variables in this chapter including declaring them and assigning values to them. We'll get some experience with variables that have an `Object` data type. We won't go into too much detail on classes until we cover that aspect of Java later on in the text so some of the material you will have to take for granted for the time being. Let's take a look at how variables work in the Java programming language.

Data Types

What is a data type? Recall from our previous discussions about programming languages and Java. We specified that Java was a strongly typed language and that this meant Java "cared" about the type of each variable and doesn't allow us to arbitrarily change the type of a variable or assign a value of an incompatible type to that variable.

That's a really complicated way of saying that a given variable will only hold one type of data. Now, even as I say this, there are features of Java that allow you to have dynamically typed variables that accept different types of data sort of similar to the way variables work in JavaScript. Once you understand how statically typed variables work, you can easily begin working with dynamic typed variables using the var keyword. We'll cover them in the advanced section.

V. G. Brusca, *Introduction to Java Through Game Development*, https://doi.org/10.1007/978-1-4842-8951-8_3

But what is a type of data? Well, this is a more complicated question to answer. A type of data is just that, data that has certain characteristics. In our case, we're talking about data that could be a single value like an account number or a complex object that holds multiple pieces of information using different data types. You could also define a series of values using an array data type. We'll begin by looking at the Java programming language's basic data types.

Basic Data Types

One of the fundamental building blocks of any Java program is variables. Variables in Java, as we mentioned earlier, are typed, and as such, there are a set of data types that are considered to be the basic data types of the Java programming language.

They are only basic in the sense that they are fundamental to the language and not class based. Mainly they are used to represent simple data like numeric values, totals, sums, words, names, descriptions, etc. A good analogy when thinking about variables is to think of them as the input on a web form. We've all filled out countless forms online.

When you enter your name into a text field on a web page, you can think of this as assigning the value of your name to a variable meant to store that name. Since your name is a series of characters (in Java, we call this a string), we would expect to use a variable of type String to store the data. Listing 3-1 shows how this variable would be expressed in Java.

Listing 3-1. Example of a String Variable

```
1 String name;
```

An example of a string variable that could hold a person's name.

With that concept in mind, let's take a look at the different basic data types available to us in the Java programming language.

We'll also include some information about each data type and an example variable declaration. All of this is shown subsequently in Table 3-1.

Table 3-1. *The Basic Data Types of the Java Programming Language*

Name	Type	Min	Max (Inclusive)	Example
Boolean	A binary, true/false, value	n/a (0 or false)	n/a (1 or true)	boolean b;
Byte	An 8-bit whole number value	-128	127	byte b;
Short	A 16-bit whole number value	-32,768	32,767	short s;
int	A 32-bit whole number value	-2 E 31	2 E 31 – 1	int i;
long	A 64-bit whole number value	-2 E 63	2 E 63 – 1	long l;
float	A real number with IEEE 754 32-bit precision	1.4 E -45	3.4028235 E 38	float f;
double	A real number with IEEE 754 64-bit precision	4.9 E -324	1.7976931348623157 E 308	double d;
char	A single Unicode character	'\u0000' (0)	'\uffff' (65,535)	char c;
String	A series of Unicode characters	0 (empty string)	Max string length supported by the JRE on the given system or 2147483647 characters	String s;

The set of basic data types in the Java programming language.

Don't allow the table of data to overwhelm you. There's really not too much going on here. Think of these as the basic tools you have for describing data in your programs. Some you will use more often than others. At times many may seem like a good choice. It will take some experience solving problems with Java before you will be able to quickly and confidently decide what data type your variable should be. And even then, it can be difficult to decide. In general, I would suggest using a data type that supports the data you expect to store in the given variable and no more.

For instance, if you were storing bank account values, you could probably get away with using floats. Very few people will achieve the kind of wealth that would require a double data type. Let's work through a general thought process when determining what data type to use. Do you need decimal-level precision? If not, then you can ignore float and double. If you aren't storing a character or a string, then you can ignore char and string data types. That leaves you with byte, short, int, and long.

Chances are long is too big, in very few cases do we need to work with numbers this large. Byte is very small. You only need to work with bytes when you're working with binary data; shorts and ints will suffice in most cases. However, shorts have a small max value that's kind of limiting. It's not so large so it can't be easily overcome numerically speaking.

That would put us in an awkward position because our variable would cease to do its job properly. It would not be able to track numbers outside the range of a short. In this little thought experiment, we would most likely settle on using an int. If you had a reason to choose another basic data type, you would have come to that point when factoring the use of that data type, as we've done here.

Boolean data types come in handy when you want to track the occurrence of something. There are many occasions in a program, video games included, where you will set a Boolean variable to true or false to indicate the existence of some situation, value, state, etc. The use of these variables stands out because you only need to indicate a change with a value. If you can replace the variable with an integer and use 0 and 1 to represent false and true, respectively, then that variable should probably use a Boolean data type.

That's all I want to cover for the introduction to basic variables. We'll get some experience using them in just a moment when we encounter the chapter's coding challenges. Let's take a look at how to use basic data-typed variables.

Using Basic Data Types

Although they are basic data types, as I mentioned earlier, they are fundamental to any Java program. We've seen, in the previous section, how to declare variables using the basic data types. I'll summarize the use of the basic data types in variable declaration in Listing 3-2.

Listing 3-2. Variable Declaration and the Basic Data Types

```
1 boolean b;
2 byte b;
3 short s;
4 int i;
```

```
5 long l;
6 float f;
7 double d;
8 char c;
9 String s;
```

An example of a variable declaration using Java's basic data types. In its simplest form, variable declaration is the data type keyword followed by the variable name.

Java Programming Note: *Take the time to give your variables meaningful names when they are important higher-level variables. Use short names, like those shown previously, for temporary variables.*

The pattern for basic variable declaration is the data type keyword followed by a valid variable name. Next, let's cover initialization of a declared variable. Notice that the data must match the data type. Some casting, conversion, is allowed between similar data types, but we won't cover this advanced topic here. Let's take a look at Listing 3-3.

Listing 3-3. Variable Declaration with Initialization and the Basic Data Types

```
01 boolean b;
02 b = true;
03
04 byte b;
05 b = 0;
06
07 short s;
08 s = 256;
09
10 int i;
11 i = -1;
12
13 long l;
14 l = 32000000;
15
16 float f;
```

```
17 f = 1.3f;
18
19 double d;
20 d = 2e15;
21
22 char c;
23 c = 'c';
24
25 String s;
26 s = "some string here";
```

An example of a variable declaration and initialization using Java's basic data types.

**Java Programming Note: When initializing variables, it's best to follow the same paradigm set out by the current code in the program, if any. If the program is new, then keep a consistent approach to variable declaration and initialization.*

There is also a shorter form of declaration and initialization referred to as instantiation. Normally, this notion would only apply to objects and classes but the syntax for basic data types is similar, so I loosely refer to it as instantiation. An example of instantiation with all the basic data types is shown in Listing 3-4.

Listing 3-4. Variable Instantiation and the Basic Data Types

```
1 boolean b = true;
2 byte b = 0;
3 short s = 256;
4 int i = -1;
5 long l = 32000000;
6 float f = 1.3f;
7 double d = 2e15;
8 char c = 'c';
9 String s = "some string here";
```

An example of a variable instantiation using Java's basic data types.

As you can see, the use of variables, of the basic data type, in Java is very straightforward. Don't be disarmed by this simplicity; it's very powerful. You can do quite a lot with variables of this type alone. But there are still more data types we must look at. Java is a robust language with a full set of features. Before we get to this though, let's tackle a coding challenge to reinforce the material we've covered on variables and basic data types.

Challenge: Basic Data Types

Welcome to your first coding challenge. Each coding challenge will involve some introduction or setup and involve a special copy of one of the included video games specifically configured with a code challenge on the given Java programming topic. This copy of the game will exist in a special package that indicates the chapter and the number of the challenge in that chapter.

Following the package that holds the coding challenge will be one that holds the solution. We'll also cover the solution in the text, but it's always best to look at the code and get experience reading and interpreting Java statements. Here is your first challenge:

Packages Involved:

```
net.middlemind.PongClone_Chapter3_Challenge1
net.middlemind.PongClone_Chapter3_Challenge1_Solved
```

Description:

Find the package, net.middlemind.PongClone_Chapter3_Challenge1, and open the PongClone.java file. This version of the game accidentally had a bug introduced after testing. An inadvertent key strike has altered a variable value and broken the game. Your challenge is to find the variable that has the incorrect value and fix it. You must run this file – PongClone.java – right-click and select Run File to test the game.

Image 3-1. *The Broken Version of This Challenge's Game*

A screenshot of the copy of the game used in this challenge. It crashes on the loading screen.

Clue:

The Pong Clone video game uses a game "engine config file," this is a hint, to data drive some aspects of the game's configuration. The null pointer exception that the game throws when loading is caused by a game engine configuration error.

Take a moment to try out the challenge. Hint, tracing the exception won't help you in this case because the resource not being loaded doesn't cause an exception at the source of the problem. It seems tricky, but it is perhaps deceptively simple. Give it a try before moving on to read the solution. Remember that the challenges take place in their own sandbox, a special package for the challenge.

In order to run this package's specific version of the game, you have to click on the static main class contained in the package and select "Run File" from the context menu. Otherwise, the project's default game will execute. If you've solved the challenge correctly, the game should run properly.

Challenge Solution

The solution to the challenge can be found in the following package:

`net.middlemind.PongClone_Chapter3_Challenge1_Solved`

Specifically in the PongClone.java file. You can search for the text, "CHAPTER 3 CHALLENGE 1 SOLUTION", to find the solution code and an explanation. I will also briefly discuss the solution here. In this case, almost the exact name of the variable that needs to be adjusted is given in the description of the challenge, "engine config file", which becomes "ENGINE_CONFIG_FILE". The word "file" also gave us a clue because there are not many file names in the variable declaration section.

To correct the issue, all you need to do is adjust the value of the `ENGINE_CONFIG_FILE` variable so that it matches the name of the file on the file system. In this case, the name should be "engine_config_mmg_pong_clone.xml" instead of "engine_config_mmg_png_clone.xml", which is missing an "o". This may seem like a silly example for a challenge, but it actually has some interesting attributes to it.

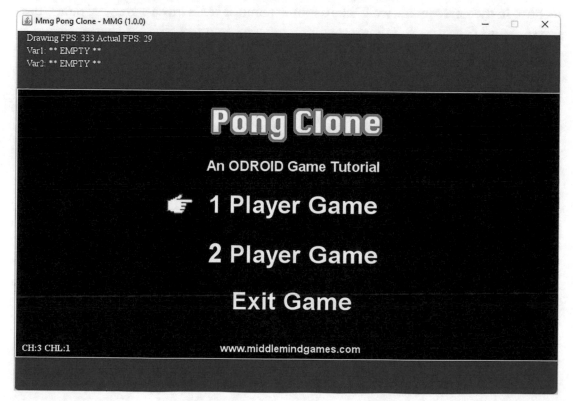

Image 3-2. *The Working Version of This Challenge's Game*

A screenshot of the fixed version of the game for this challenge.

**Game Programming Note: Games and game engines frequently have complex subsystem responsible for loading different resources. It's often important to take the time to get to know these systems so that you can competently triage any related bugs during development.*

For one, the error was not directly tied to the solution. It took some knowledge of the game engine to understand what the error really meant. From the perspective of the JRE, there is a null value, and an exception should be thrown. But from the perspective of the video game, there is a null value because a resource didn't load. Either the missing resource was not specified properly or it doesn't exist. Barring the nonexistence case, we are left with a configuration-driven, resource-loading issue.

This points us directly at the game engine config file where we would look to see what configuration exists for the given game. That brings us to the conclusion of this section. In the next section, we'll take a look at some of Java's more advanced data types and their use.

Advanced Data Types

You can do a lot with just the basic data types, but Java has even more power to offer you as a developer. There are a few advanced data types that we should look at. These include a dynamic data type, as opposed to the static typing, we are used to. There are even some data types that help us define sets of data which we'll also take a look at here.

The var Keyword and Dynamic Typing

Despite all my tough talk about Java's rigorous, strong typing, the language actually supports dynamic typing. The var keyword, introduced in Java 10, uses data type inference in which it automatically detects the data type of a variable based on the surrounding context. This is a fairly advanced use of Java. We won't go into too much detail here. There are a number of rules governing the use of the var keyword in the Java programming language.

For simplicity's sake, I'm going to generalize and oversimplify its use. If you feel comfortable exploring further, you can find more information here:

`www.geeksforgeeks.org/var-keyword-in-java/`

As I stated earlier, the var keyword allows you to use dynamic typing with a variable. You can declare a variable of type var in a few places, but for our purposes, we'll limit its use to inside a method. I should also mention that variable data type redefinition is not supported. This means that Java will detect the data type for the var variable only the first time it is initialized. Subsequent assignments must adhere to the first detected data type. Allow me to advance this notion with an example shown in Listing 3-5.

Listing 3-5. Variable Instantiation and the var Data Type

```
01 public static void main(String[] args) {
02     //int
03     var x = 100;
04
05     //double
06     var y = 1.90;
07
08     //char
09     var z = 'a';
10
11     //string
12     var p = "tanu";
13
14     //boolean
15     var q = false;
16 }
```

An example showing the use of the var data type with variable instantiation.

I'd also like to take a moment and demonstrate an incorrect usage of the var data type. In Listing 3-6, we'll demonstrate redefining the data type of a var variable, which will cause an exception to be thrown. Let's take a look.

Listing 3-6. Variable Data Type Redefinition and the var Data Type

```
1 //the compiler interprets the variable as an int
2 var id = 0;
3
4 //error thrown because of incompatible data types
5 id = "34";
```

An example showing the use of the var data type with variable data type redefinition error.

You can see from the example that the var keyword sort of acts as a placeholder for an unknown basic data type that is inferred when the variable is initialized. It sounds complicated, but if you think about it for a moment, it's just like using the other basic data types, only in a roundabout way. You're letting the data drive the variable's data type instead of explicitly setting it when the variable is declared. Pretty neat!

Ok, so after that whole section on the var data type and its use, I'm sad to inform you that we won't be doing a challenge with this material. It's just that I personally don't use this feature very much and I rather enjoy the stricter approach to variables that the traditional data types offer. In the next section, we'll take a look at another advanced data type and our first "data structure": the array.

Arrays

Up until this point, we've been working with variables that are used to keep track of one value, and we've mainly been using basic data types. A common occurrence in problem solving is the concept of sets of data. Any series of tests will give a series of scores. It becomes arduous to have to name and define a new variable to track each and every value in cases like this.

Allow me to further this notion with another example, the results from a test given to a group of students in a classroom. In this case, we have two sets of data to track: the students and the test results. Now, using the knowledge we currently have about the Java programming language, we could add a new variable for each student and one for each student's test results.

This would be possible but would quickly become an untenable program to use and/or manage. You would have so many variables to keep track of that it would quickly become a self-defeating solution. Fear not, we have the array to rely on to streamline this type of data representation, namely, groups of similar data of a known size.

An array is a special type of variable that contains other variables. It can be thought of as an object that holds a fixed number of values of a single data type. The length of an array is set when the array is created and remains fixed. You can manually resize an array by reinitializing it, but there is no automatic process for doing so. There are other data types to use in those circumstances. We'll take a look at some of them soon.

Let's take a look at how to declare an array. In Listing 3-7, we'll demonstrate the code necessary to declare an array of the basic data types we've just finished reviewing.

Listing 3-7. Array Declaration and the Basic Data Types + 1

```
01 boolean[] arrayOfBooleans;
02 byte[] arrayOfBytes;
03 short[] arrayOfShorts;
04 int[] arrayOfInts;
05 long[] arrayOfLongs;
06 float[] arrayOfFloats;
07 double[] arrayOfDoubles;
08 char[] arrayOfChars;
09 String[] arrayOfStrings;
10 Object[] arrayOfObjects;
```

An example showing the code used to declare an array of the basic data types and one additional data type, the Object type.

As you can see, it's not much different from the variable declarations we've seen previously. Notice the use of the brackets, [ ]; these indicate that the variable is going to be an array of the type listed. The reason for this is because brackets are also used to reference a particular element in an array. In this way, they are sort of synonymous with arrays in the Java programming language, so using them to indicate that the declared variable is an array of a specified type is intuitive.

You may have noticed that the last entry in the listing isn't an array of a basic data type. This is an early introduction to an object. Java is an object-oriented programming language that supports the creation of custom objects by creating a class definition for that object. All of this is a bit much to discuss this early on. For now, think of the `Object` data type as the parent of all objects that are created in Java. In the next section, we will look at how you initialize and use arrays.

Using Arrays

Using arrays is a little bit more complicated than the basic data types we've worked with thus far, but there are strong similarities in how you use them, in fact, in how you use any variable in Java. In the previous section, we saw how you can declare an array. This is similar to the declaration of a variable of a basic data type with the exception that arrays are data structures.

Previous variables we looked at were variables that stored a single value. Arrays, however, are designed to hold many values. But as you might expect, this requires some initialization. For instance, you may be asking how many values does an array hold? Good question. It's your choice up to the maximum value of the integer data type or until you run out of memory, whichever comes first.

In any case, you should create arrays with a size designed to work with the data that the array is intended to hold. If you're creating a representation of the days of the week, then you could use an array of length seven. You get the idea. Let's take a look at declaration and instantiation of different arrays of basic data types and the Object data type. Why not. Take a look at Listing 3-8 for the demonstration code.

Listing 3-8. Array Declaration and Initialization of the Basic Data Types + 1

```
01 boolean[] arrayOfBooleans;
02 arrayOfBooleans = new boolean[10];
03
04 byte[] arrayOfBytes;
05 arrayOfBytes = new byte[10];
06
07 short[] arrayOfShorts;
08 arrayOfShorts = new short[10];
09
10 int[] arrayOfInts;
11 arrayOfInts = new int[10];
12
13 long[] arrayOfLongs;
14 arrayOfLongs = new long[10];
15
16 float[] arrayOfFloats;
```

```
17 arrayOfFloats = new float[10];
18
19 double[] arrayOfDoubles;
20 arrayOfDoubles = new double[10];
21
22 char[] arrayOfChars;
23 arrayOfChars = new char[10];
24
25 String[] arrayOfStrings;
26 arrayOfStrings = new String[10];
27
28 Object[] arrayOfObjects;
29 arrayOfObjects = new Object[10];
```

An example showing the code used to declare and initialize an array of the basic data types and one additional data type, the Object type.

There's a slightly shorter way to accomplish the same thing, shown in Listing 3-9.

Listing 3-9. Array Instantiation of the Basic Data Types + 1

```
01 boolean[] arrayOfBooleans = new boolean[10];
02 byte[] arrayOfBytes = new byte[10];
03 short[] arrayOfShorts = new short[10];
04 int[] arrayOfInts = new int[10];
05 long[] arrayOfLongs = new long[10];
06 float[] arrayOfFloats = new float[10];
07 double[] arrayOfDoubles = new double[10];
08 char[] arrayOfChars = new char[10];
09 String[] arrayOfStrings = new String[10];
10 Object[] arrayOfObjects = new Object[10];
```

An example showing the code used to instantiate an array of the basic data types and one additional data type, the Object type.

There may be certain circumstances where you have all of the data you need for the array right at the start. This often happens with short arrays of static, common data like the days of the week, months of the year, etc. Let's take a look at this version of array instantiation next in Listing 3-10.

Listing 3-10. Array Instantiation with Element Initialization of the Basic Data Types + 1

```
01 boolean[] bools = new boolean[]{false, true};
02 byte[] bytes = new byte[]{0, 1, 2, 3};
03 short[] shorts = new short[]{1024, 2048};
04 int[] ints = new int[]{10, 20, 30};
05 long[] longs = new long[]{2e24, 2e18};
06 float[] floats = new float[]{1.01, 1.02};
07 double[] doubles = new double[]{1.03, 1.04};
08 char[] chars = new char[]{'a', 'b', 'c'};
09 String[] strings = new String[]{"hello", "world"};
10 Object[] objects = new Object[]{new Object()};
```

An example showing the code used to instantiate an array with element initialization of the basic data types and one additional data type, the Object type.

**Java Programming Note: *You should only use this type of array declaration with a small amount of data. If you have more than just a few items, think about how you could data drive loading the array elements instead.*

**Game Programming Note: *While arrays can be thought of as antiquated and error prone when building games, using tightly controlled arrays can be much faster than other data structures. But the speed comes at the cost of static length and an increased potential for errors.*

In this case, we know what values we want to set for the array, so when we instantiate the array, we can list those elements explicitly. In this way, not only are we initializing the array, we are also initializing the array's elements. This is an important distinction to make between the code shown in Listing 3-10 and previous two listings, Listings 3-8 and 3-9. So what exactly is going on? We're initializing an array and its elements. What does that mean?

Well let me explain by going back a little bit. When you declare a variable, you don't necessarily have to set its value. This is the distinction between declaration, initialization, and instantiation. We use the term "instantiation" here loosely. It actually applies more to the use of objects, but I like to maintain this distinction with all data types.

Declaration: Basic variables are ready to use with a default value, while objects are null and not ready to use.

```
int i;      //default value set to 0
Object o;   //default value set to null
```

Declaration followed by initialization: Basic variables are ready to use and are initialized to a specific value. For Variables with an Object data type, a new instance of the object is created and initialized by using the "new" keyword.

```
int i;
i = 2;                  //ready to use
Object o;
o = new Object();   //ready to use
```

Instantiation: Basic variables are ready to use and initialized to a specific value. Variables with an Object data type, a new instance of the object is created and initialized by using the "new" keyword.

```
int i = 2;                  //ready to use
Object o = new Object();   //ready to use
```

With regard to arrays, the same rules apply, but you must stop and think about what an array is. It's a data structure that stores a series of values all of the same data type. It has a fixed length, and you can access each element in the array by using its index. The array indexing starts at 0 and ends at array length – 1. Let's look at what declaration, initialization, and instantiation look like for arrays.

Declaration: The array is null and not ready to use.

```
int[] i;         //default value set to null
Object[] o;      //default value set to null
```

Declaration followed by initialization: The array is ready to use. Arrays of basic data types are ready to use with each element set to a default value, while arrays of objects are not ready to use as each array element is still null. This is an important distinction.

```
int[] i;
i = new int[10];      //ready to use
Object[] o;
o = new Object[10];   //ready to use
```

Instantiation: The array is ready to use. Arrays of basic data types are ready to use with each element set to a default value, while arrays of objects are not ready to use as each array element is null.

```
int[] i = new int[10];            //ready to use
Object[] o = new Object[10];  //elements set to null
```

Explicit array instantiation: The array is ready to use. Arrays of basic data types are ready to use with each element set to a specific value. Arrays of objects are ready to use as each array element is set to a new instance of an object.

```
int[] i = new int[]{10, 20, 30};                          //ready to use
Object[] o = new Object[]{new Object(), new Object()}; //ready to use
```

It is important to realize when it may be dangerous to use an array element because it has not been initialized. Now that we've seen how to declare and initialize an array, let's take a look at how you can access, get and set, the elements of an array (Listing 3-11).

Listing 3-11. Array Element Access – Get and Set

```
1 boolean[] bools = new boolean[]{false, true};
2
3 //flip the values
4 bool b = bools[0];
5 bools[0] = bools[1];
6 bools[1] = b;
```

A small code snippet showing how to get and set elements of an array by their index.

That was pretty easy. As long as you know the index of an array element, you can get or set its value. You have to always use a value of the same, or compatible, data type as that of the array or you will get an error. One aspect of arrays that is particularly useful is the length of the array. Now, you could keep track of the array's length in a variable:

```
int len = 10;
int[] a = new int[len];
```

This can get a bit cumbersome, so the array object in Java has an attribute to help you with this; the length attribute is shown in Listing 3-12.

Listing 3-12. Array Length Attribute

```
//code
1 int[] i = new int[10];
2 System.out.println("Array Length Is: " + i.length);

//output
1 Array Length Is: 10
```

A tiny snippet of code that demonstrated using the array's length attribute.

You will see the length attribute a lot when we take a look at looping in Java. It comes in handy when iterating over the contents of an array. You might be wondering how do you copy an array? Well, you might think that the following would do the trick:

```
int[] a = new int[] {0, 1, 2};
int[] b = new int[] {4, 5, 6};
b = a;
```

This is more of a topic to be discussed during the review of Java's object-oriented programming support. We may as well touch upon it since we're here. Java uses a concept called a reference. These are applied to all objects including arrays in the language. In this way, a and b are variables, but they are references to array objects.

When you try to copy a reference, it simply changes what the new variable points to. So while it may seem as if you've made a copy of integer array a, you've actually created two variables that reference the same array in memory, a and b. We can demonstrate this in Listing 3-14.

Listing 3-13. Array Copy – Creating a Reference to an Array

```
//code1 int[] a = new int[] {1, 2, 3};
2 int[] b = new int[] {4, 5, 6};
3
4 b = a;
5 System.out.println("Array b Element 0: " + b[0]);
6
7 a[0] = -1;
8 System.out.println("Array b Element 0: " + b[0]);
```

```
//output
1 Array b Element 0: 1
2 Array b Element 0: -1
```

An example of creating two variables that reference the same array.

We can tell that b is a reference to the same array as variable a because when we change the first element of a, line 7, and print out the first element of b, the value changes. Again, we'll cover this in more detail when it's the proper time. For now, though, I'd like to show you two techniques that you can use to copy arrays, which actually work, in Listing 3-14.

Listing 3-14. Array Copy – Creating an Independent Copy of an Array

```
//code
01 int[] a = new int[] {1, 2, 3};
02 int[] b = new int[] {4, 5, 6};
03
04 //old copy
05 //b = a;
06
07 //new copy
08 for(int i = 0; i < b.length; i++) {
09     if(i >= 0 && i < a.length) {
10         b[i] = a[i];
11         //for objects you would use something like this
12         //b[i] = a[i].clone();
13         //to create a unique copy of the elements
14     }
15 }
16
17 System.out.println("Array b Element 0: " + b[0]);
18
19 a[0] = -1;
20 System.out.println("Array b Element 0: " + b[0]);

//output
01 Array b Element 0: 1
02 Array b Element 0: 1
```

An example of creating an independent copy of an array of type int.

You can also use the System class' arraycopy method to copy data from one array to another. The signature for the method is as follows:

```
public static void arraycopy(Object src, int srcPos, Object dest, int
destPos, int length)
```

Notice that the src and dest method arguments are of the Object data type and not one of the array data types we've seen thus far. The reason for this is because an array is an instance of an Object. We'll discuss this more when we cover objects and classes. I feel like I'm saying that a lot.

But in all seriousness, this solution to copying arrays shows that an array, int[ ], is an instance of an Object in the Java programming language. Then you can perform the same array copy as the code in Listing 3-14 like so:

```
System.arraycopy(a, 0, b, 0, 3);
```

Lastly, in order to use an array properly, you need to know how to delete one. In its simplest form, you can clear out an array with the following line of code:

```
some_valid_array = null;
```

However, if you are working with an array of objects and you want to make sure those objects are also deleted, you can explicitly set each array element to null like so:

```
for(int i = 0; i < b.length; i++) {
    b[i] = null;
}
```

That brings us to the conclusion of the section. There are many more ways that you can use an array in terms of the logic of certain algorithms, but as far as Java programming is concerned, you have all the basics covered and some insight into advanced topics. In the next section, we'll take on our second coding challenge. Let's jump into some code!

Challenge: Arrays

The second challenge in this chapter requires you to make three small changes to the specified Java file. Using your new knowledge of arrays, you should be able to accomplish the requirements of this challenge. Here are the details:

Packages Involved:

```
net.middlemind.PongClone_Chapter3_Challenge2
net.middlemind.PongClone_Chapter3_Challenge2_Solved
```

Description:

Find the package, net.middlemind.PongClone_Chapter3_Challenge2, and open the ScreenGame.java file. In this challenge, the second one in this chapter, we'll look at a version of the Pong Clone game that needs a slight adjustment. The lead developer doesn't like so many Switch statements in the DrawScreen method.

They would like to remove the Switch statements for the SHOW_COUNT_DOWN_IN_GAME and SHOW_COUNT_DOWN game states and replace them with if-else statements that test an array value. The new code is ready in the DrawScreen method, but it is currently commented out. You need to define and initialize a new integer array called "numbers" with a length of 4. This array should be initialized with each value in the NumberState enumeration. Use the following statements to get the integer values for the elements of the array:

- NumberState.NONE.ordinal()

- NumberState.NUMBER_1.ordinal()

- NumberState.NUMBER_2.ordinal()

- NumberState.NUMBER_3.ordinal()

You can initialize the array in any way that works, but it is recommended you use the LoadResources method. You must run this package's file - PongClone.java; right-click and select Run File to test the game.

Clue:

Here are some clues to help you with the challenge. If you are unsure about what values to set for the numbers array, take a look at the commented-out new code in the DrawScreen method. If you're concerned about where to place your initialization code in the LoadResources method, use a spot near the end of the method.

In order to run the package's specific version of the game, you have to click on the static main class contained in that package and select "Run File" from the context menu. Otherwise, the project's default game will execute. If you've solved the challenge correctly, the game should run properly.

Challenge Solution

The solution to this challenge requires you to make three small changes to the challenge package's ScreenGame.java file. The first change is to declare a new array of integers with the name "numbers." This is usually done at the top of a Java file, but you should follow the convention already in place in the file if any. The second change to the file you must make is to initialize the array. It is recommended to add this code to the LoadResources method so that we follow the convention of initializing objects in the same place.

The last change you have to make to the file is to remove the comments around the new code and add multi-line comments, /* */, to the old code. Once this is done, you can run the PongClone.java class for this challenge package and test your changes. This challenge is a little anticlimactic in that a correct solution would show no change from the previous implementation. It turns out this is a common occurrence in the real world.

A screenshot showing the refactored countdown code working properly.

If you run into trouble, you can check out the solution code and comments in the associated solution package. In the next section, we'll take a sneak peek at another data type: the List data structure.

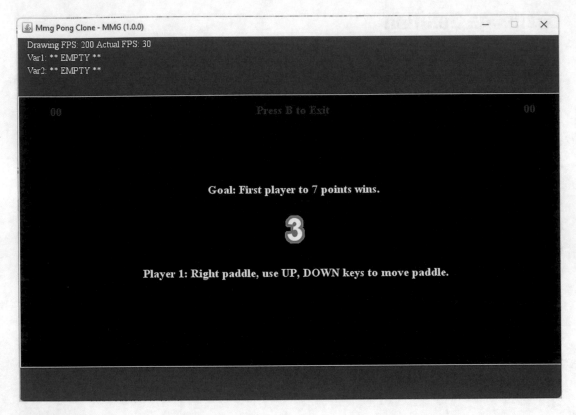

Image 3-3. *A Correct Solution with Working Countdown*

Lists

It is perhaps a bit premature to start dealing with data structures of any complexity, but I want you to be a functional Java developer at the completion of this text. To this end, I would like to quickly review Lists in a simple and direct way that demonstrates a common use case: the dynamic array. When working with data structures other than arrays, you'll most likely need to include Java's data structures package, like so:

```
import java.util.*
```

This will give you access to Java's data structure classes in your program. You don't have to understand everything that's going on here with regard to objects and methods, but you should understand what's going on with regard to using a list as a dynamically sized replacement for an array. Let's take a look at some ways to declare a list (Listing 3-15).

Listing 3-15. Declaring Lists – Basic Data Types + 1

```
1 ArrayList<Boolean> listBooleans;
2 ArrayList<Byte> listBytes;
3 ArrayList<Short> listShorts;
4 ArrayList<Integer> listIntegers;
5 ArrayList<Long> listLongs;
6 ArrayList<Float> listFloats;
7 ArrayList<Double> listDoubles;
8 ArrayList listObjects1;
9 ArrayList<Object> listObject2;
```

An example of declaring lists of the basic data types plus the object type. Note the different ways to use an Object as the List data type on lines 8 and 9.

Note that we're using Java's ArrayList class, which is an implementation of a List. Also, notice that the declaration of lists doesn't use the actual basic data types. It uses an object version of them. Defining the data type of the list is done with the angle bracket operator, <>. When no data type is specified, the default, Object, is used. Next, let's take a look at the long form of initialization for the ArrayList class.

Listing 3-16. Declaring and Initializing Lists – Basic Data Types + 1

```
01 ArrayList<Boolean> listBooleans;
02 listBooleans = new ArrayList();
03
04 ArrayList<Byte> listBytes;
05 listBytes = new ArrayList();
06
07 ArrayList<Short> listShorts;
08 listShorts = new ArrayList();
09
10 ArrayList<Integer> listIntegers;
11 listIntegers = new ArrayList();
12
13 ArrayList<Long> listLongs;
14 listLongs = new ArrayList();
15
```

```
16 ArrayList<Float> listFloats;
17 listFloats = new ArrayList();
18
19 ArrayList<Double> listDoubles;
20 listDoubles = new ArrayList();
21
22 ArrayList listObjects1;
23 listObjects1 = new ArrayList();
24
25 ArrayList<Object> listObjects2;
26 listObjects2 = new ArrayList();
```

An example of the long form of declaring and initializing lists of the basic data types plus the object type.

You can instantiate a new instance of a list using the following Java statements. This is a more concise version of the declare and initialize code we just looked at.

Listing 3-17. Instantiating Lists – Basic Data Types + 1

```
1 ArrayList<Boolean> listBooleans = new ArrayList();
2 ArrayList<Byte> listBytes = new ArrayList();
3 ArrayList<Short> listShorts = new ArrayList();
4 ArrayList<Integer> listIntegers = new ArrayList();
5 ArrayList<Long> listLongs = new ArrayList();
6 ArrayList<Float> listFloats = new ArrayList();
7 ArrayList<Double> listDoubles = new ArrayList();
8 ArrayList listObjects1 = new ArrayList();
9 ArrayList<Object> listObjects2 = new ArrayList();
```

An example of the short form of declaring and initializing lists of the basic data types plus the object type.

This code should be familiar. It's very similar to the array code we reviewed previously. In the next section, we'll take a look at how you actually use a list. Keep in mind that at no point in the initialization code did we set a size for the lists. One of the main features of lists is that they can grow in size as needed. Awesome! Let's explore further.

Using Lists

The first thing we'll look at in this section is how to get and set elements in a list, specifically Java's ArrayList object. Let's look at the same code we used in the section on using arrays except we'll adjust the code to work specifically for ArrayLists. Let's take a look at Listing 3-18.

Listing 3-18. ArrayList Element Access – Get and Set

```
1 ArrayList<Boolean> bools = new ArrayList();
2 bools.add(Boolean.FALSE);
3 bools.add(Boolean.TRUE);
4
5 //flip the values
6 Boolean b = bools.get(0);
7 bools.set(0, bools.get(1));
8 bools.set(1, b);
```

Code snippet showing an ArrayList having two elements flipped demonstrating how to get and set values.

Notice that the code is very similar, except that we use explicit methods, get and set, to interact with the list elements instead of array index notation, [ ]. Also take a moment to note how we use the object version of the boolean basic data type. Because lists require objects for elements, we are forced to use the Java objects that "box" their corresponding basic data types.

Converting between basic data types and their corresponding object equivalents is referred to as boxing and unboxing. More on this to come. Let's take a look at some important methods of the ArrayList class in Listing 3-19.

Listing 3-19. ArrayList – Important Methods

```
//code
1 ArrayList<Boolean> bools = new ArrayList();
2 bools.add(Boolean.FALSE);
3 bools.add(Boolean.TRUE);
4
5 System.out.println("ArrayList Size: " + bools.size());
6 System.out.println("ArrayList IsEmpty: " + bools.isEmpty());
```

```
//output
1 ArrayList Size: 2
2 ArrayList IsEmpty: false
```

Code snippet showing some important ArrayList methods in use.

Another useful action to perform with ArrayLists is to copy them. The code is a bit different than with arrays:

```
ArrayList<Boolean> newBools = new ArrayList(bools);
```

Using the array, bools, from the previous listing, we can create a copy of it by initializing a new ArrayList and using the previous one as an argument. You could also manually copy the ArrayList elements as shown in Listing 3-20.

Listing 3-20. ArrayList – Copy List Using Initialization

```
//code
01 ArrayList<Boolean> bools = new ArrayList();
02 bools.add(Boolean.FALSE);
03 bools.add(Boolean.TRUE);
04
05 System.out.println("Bools ArrayList Size: " + bools.size());
06 System.out.println("Bools ArrayList IsEmpty: " + bools.isEmpty());
07
08 ArrayList<Boolean> newBools = new ArrayList(bools);

09 System.out.println("NewBools ArrayList Size: " + newBools.size());
10 System.out.println("NewBools ArrayList IsEmpty: " + newBools.isEmpty());
```

```
//output
Bools ArrayList Size: 2
Bools ArrayList IsEmpty: false
NewBools ArrayList Size: 2
NewBools ArrayList IsEmpty: false
```

An example of how to copy an ArrayList using initialization.

There's more than one way to copy an ArrayList. Listing 3-21 demonstrates copying one using an explicit approach.

Listing 3-21. ArrayList – Copy List Using Explicit Add

```
//code
01 ArrayList<Boolean> bools = new ArrayList();
02 bools.add(Boolean.FALSE);
03 bools.add(Boolean.TRUE);
04
05 System.out.println("Bools ArrayList Size: " + bools.size());
06 System.out.println("Bools ArrayList IsEmpty: " + bools.isEmpty());
07
08 ArrayList<Boolean> newBools = new ArrayList();
09 for(int i = 0; i < newBools.size(); i++) {
10     if(i < bools.size()) {
11         newBools.add(bools.get(i));
12     }
13 }
14
15 System.out.println("NewBools ArrayList Size: " + newBools.size());
16 System.out.println("NewBools ArrayList IsEmpty: " + newBools.isEmpty());

//output
01 Bools ArrayList Size: 2
02 Bools ArrayList IsEmpty: false
03 NewBools ArrayList Size: 2
04 NewBools ArrayList IsEmpty: false
```

An example of how to copy an ArrayList using explicit add.

The second approach gives you more control over how you copy the list elements. Notice that we're using the same code as before; we've just replaced the part that handles copying the list. This last little snippet of code shows us how to delete an `ArrayList` (Listing 3-22).

Listing 3-22. Deleting an ArrayList

```
//code
1 ArrayList<Boolean> bools = new ArrayList();
2 bools.add(Boolean.FALSE);
3 bools.add(Boolean.TRUE);
```

```
4 bools.clear();
5 bools = null;
```

A code snippet demonstrating how to delete an ArrayList by clearing it before setting it to null.

**Java Programming Note: Take the time to properly manage your data structures and elements. Just because Java has a garbage collector that cleans up unused memory for us doesn't mean we have to give it a lot of work to do.

When we were dealing with arrays, there was a concept of keeping track of both the initialization of the array and that of its elements. The same applies when using ArrayLists. In the next section, we'll tackle one last challenge that'll test our knowledge of ArrayLists.

Challenge: ArrayLists

In this challenge, the last one in this chapter, we'll gain some more experience working with the Pong Clone game's main screen, ScreenGame.java. In this challenge, we'll be tasked with refactoring the current code while maintaining the functionality of the game. We'll be using our newly acquired ArrayList knowledge to do so. Let's take a look.

Packages Involved:

```
net.middlemind.PongClone_Chapter3_Challenge3
net.middlemind.PongClone_Chapter3_Challenge3_Solved
```

Description:

Find the package, net.middlemind.PongClone_Chapter3_Challenge3, and open the ScreenGame.java file. After reviewing the changes made in the last challenge, some members of the development team want to use a data structure with a dynamic length as opposed to an array. This challenge starts with the solution from the previous challenge, so make sure you have the correct solution in place. Your challenge is to refactor the working code in this file so that the "numbers" variable is an ArrayList as opposed to an array.

You'll also have to adjust how the variable is initialized and comment out the old code while uncommenting the new code in the class' DrawScreen method. If you've done everything correctly, the game should run without error. You must run this package's file – PongClone.java; right-click and select Run File to test the game.

Clue:

Aside from commenting out the current code in the DrawScreen method that handles the SHOW_COUNT_DOWN_IN_GAME and SHOW_COUNT_DOWN game states, all you have to do is convert the numbers variable from an array to an ArrayList.

Challenge Solution

The solution to this challenge requires you to make three small changes to the challenge package's ScreenGame.java file. This file is the solution to the previous challenge, so you're working with an array of integers already. That means the code is in a state that is close to what we need. The first change to make is to alter the data type of the numbers variable from an int[] to an ArrayList.

This change will trigger a number of syntax errors at the location of the numbers variable's initialization. This code needs to be adjusted to work with lists instead of arrays. For example, "numbers[0] =" becomes "numbers.add(". This is a great example of something that will come up again and again in software development, refactoring code. It just so happens that the first implementation isn't always the best and some adjusting is needed.

Refactoring isn't an indication of a mistake or error. It's simply an indication that you're getting better at programming and have come up with a slightly different, slightly better, way of doing something. The last change to solve the challenge is to comment out the current code and uncomment the new code in the DrawScreen method.

When in doubt, check the solution package and look at the challenge file. That brings us to the end of this topic. In the next section, we'll conclude the chapter and review the material we've covered.

Conclusion

We covered a lot of material in this chapter, and we've only scratched the surface of the variable topic. We'll encounter more information as we cover more material, but this chapter constitutes a solid foundation for which to build. You already have a decent set of tools to model data in a Java program. Combine this with your ability to work with arrays and dynamic length data structures like lists and you're well on your way to mastering the language.

What We Covered

In this chapter, we reviewed the following topics on Java variables. You also got a chance to take on three challenges in this chapter, and I'll note what topics the challenges were associated with in the following list:

- Basic Data Types: In this section, we talked about the Java programming language's basic data types and how to declare variables.

- Using Basic Data Types: We got some experience working with variables and saw some examples of how to initialize variables.

- Challenge: Basic Data Types: Our first challenge which required us to fix a broken copy of the Pong Clone game.

- The var Keyword and Dynamic Typing: In this section, we explored Java's dynamic typing support via the var keyword.

- Arrays: An introduction to arrays and their declaration.

- Using Arrays: We explored how to initialize arrays and their elements and covered useful topics like copying and deleting arrays.

- Challenge: Arrays: An interesting challenge that required us to refactor the code on a copy of the Pong Clone game.

- Lists: We took it a little further than usual for an introductory text and introduced a second data type that is a data structure similar to an array: the list.

- Using Lists: We reviewed the ways in which you initialize an `ArrayList` and how to populate it with elements. We also covered useful topics like copying and deleting a list.

- Challenge ArrayLists: An interesting challenge that required us to refactor the solution to challenge #2 so that the code uses an `ArrayList` as opposed to an array.

We covered quite a bit of ground in this chapter. I hope that the use of challenges as opposed to boring example programs is an efficient way for you to get experience not only learning Java but working with the NetBeans IDE and taking on some real-world coding problems. In the next chapter, we'll take a look at the ways that we can control the flow of a program in Java.

CHAPTER 4

Expressions and Operators, Flow Control, and More on Variables

In the previous chapter, we got a fair amount of experience working with variables in Java and even took a look at more complex variables, data structures, like arrays and lists. Although our ability to model data using Java data types has increased, there's not much we can do programming-wise at this point. We need some more tools to work with.

In this chapter, we'll expand our knowledge of the Java programming language, and by doing so, we'll incorporate some more tools into our coding toolbox, as we review expressions, operators, and flow control. Using these new language features, we'll be able to combine variables and values with different operators to create expressions, and we'll also be able to control the flow of the program by combining flow control statements with Boolean expressions.

Lastly, before we conclude the chapter, we'll swing back around to the topic of variables and cover a few of the finer points on the subject like casting and custom data types. Let's jump into things and start with expressions and operators in the Java programming language!

© Victor G. Brusca 2023

V. G. Brusca, *Introduction to Java Through Game Development*, https://doi.org/10.1007/978-1-4842-8951-8_4

Expressions and Operators

As we mentioned earlier, the Java programming language has inherent support for a few main types of expressions and associated operators. Let's take a look at what the language has to offer.

- Numeric: Formulas or other numeric combinations of variables and numeric operators used to generate a number value

- Boolean: A logical expression combining variables and Boolean operators to generate a true/false value

- Assignment: Expressions used to apply an adjustment to a variable while assigning it a new value

- Increment/Decrement: A set of expressions to streamline incrementing or decrementing a variable

- Inline If-Else: An inline If-Else operator that can be used to control the variable initialization among other things

- Bit: Expressions using Java's bitwise and bit-shift operators to adjust data values and make comparisons at the bit level

In general, the operators used in expressions of these main types fall into the following categories, separated by complexity:

- Unary Operator: An operator that requires one value. Examples are the increment/decrement operators and the negative numeric operator.

- Binary Operator: An operator that requires two values. Examples are the numeric operators (+, -, /, *, %) and the Boolean operators (==, !=, <, >, <=, >=).

- Ternary Operator: A ternary operator requires three values. An example of a ternary operator is the in-line If-Else operator, "? :", which we will talk about again when we get to flow control.

Note that in Java, the "!" character is the logical complement. It converts a true value to a false value and vice versa. Another operator you might not be familiar with is the modulo operator, "%". The modulo operator is used to return the remainder after integer division. Expressions can also be categorized by their use of multiple operators, values, and even other expressions.

- Simple Expression: A basic expression that doesn't include extra operators, variables, etc. For instance, a simple expression involving a unary operator should have only that operator and the required value it's operating on.

- Compound Expression: An advanced expression that includes the use of multiple operators, variables, method calls, or other expressions.

That's a decent amount of material to take in, so before we get into the details, let's explore this topic further and discuss what exactly is an expression in the Java programming language in terms of its definition. According to the Java documentation:

"An expression is a construct made up of variables, operators, and method invocations, which are constructed according to the syntax of the language, that evaluates to a single value."

–From the official Java documentation[1]

An expression, by definition, is a construct made of lower-level language features like variables, operators, and method calls that are syntactically correct and that can be processed to provide a single result. Let's support this concept with some examples, shown in Listing 4-1. I'll provide some examples from each of the main expression types listed previously.

Listing 4-1. Examples of Different Expressions and Operators in Java

```
01 //preparation
02 ArrayList<Integer> listIntegers;
03 listIntegers = new ArrayList();
04 listIntegers.add(10);
05
06 //Simple numeric expressions
07 int i = 5;
08 i = 10;
09 i = 5 + 5;
```

[1]https://docs.oracle.com/javase/tutorial/java/nutsandbolts/expressions.html

77

```
10 i = 11 - 1;
11 i = 11 + -1;
12 i = 100 / 10;
13 i = 100 % 3;
14 i = (1 * 10);
15
16 i = 5;
17 i = i + 5;
18 i = i - +5;
19 i = i / 5;
20 i = i % 5;
21 i = (i * 5);
22
23 //simple boolean expressions
24 boolean b;
25 b = i == 5;
26 b = (j != d);     //! is the logical complement operator
27 b = (j < d);
28 b = j > listIntegers.get(0);
29 b = (j <= i);
30 b = j >= d;
31
32 //increment/decrement, negation, method use expressions
33 i = 5;
34 i++;
35 i--;
36 i = 5;
37 i = -i;
38 i = listIntegers.get(0) + 256;
39
40 //simple string expressions
41 String s;
42 s = "Hello";
43 s = s + " ";
44 s += "World";
```

```
45
46 //compound numeric expressions
47 int j;
48 double d;
49 float f;
50 i = 0 + 10 - 5;
51 j = listIntegers.get(0) + 256;
52 s = "Hello" + " " + "World!";
53 d = 10 / 2.5 + 3;
54 d = 10 * 2.5 - 3;
55 f = (float)(12.7 / 10);
56 listIntegers.set(0, 125 + j + i);
57
58 //compound boolean expressions
59 b = i + 1 == 5 + j;
60 b = (j + listIntegers.get(0) != d);
61 b = j < d + 100;
62 b = j / 2 > (listIntegers.get(0) * 2);
63 b = (j <= i++);
64 b = j >= -d;
65
66 //assignment expressions
67 i = 5;
68 i += 5;
69 i -= 5;
70 i /= 5;
71 i %= 5;
72 i *= 5;
73
74 //ternary operator, ? :, in-line If-Else
75 s = b ? "b is true" : "b is false"; //if ? then : else
76
77 //simple bit-wise expressions
78 int x, y, z; //multi-variable declaration
79 x = 5;
```

```
80 y = 7;
81 z = x | y; //bitwise OR, z = 7
82 z = x & y; //bitwise AND, z = 5
83 z = x ^ y; //bitwise XOR, z = 2
84 z = ~x; //bitwise complement, z = 10
85
86 //simple bit-shift expressions
87 byte a = 64, g;
88 i = a << 2; //i = 256
89 g = (byte)(a << 2); //i = 0 due to overflow
```

An example of each of the main expression types with associated operators. Some are shown in both a compound and a simple form.

*** Java Programming Note:** You'll notice on line 89 and line 55 that there's a data type in parentheses directly to the left of the given expression. This is called a cast, and it's used to convert the data on the right to the type specified in parentheses, if possible.*

*** Game Programming Note:** Compound expressions are fine, but if you can consolidate terms and simplify the expression, do so. A complex expression is less efficient than a simplified version of that same expression, and in game programming, it's important to strive for efficiency.*

The use of class methods in expressions is a slightly more advanced topic that belongs to the discussion on Java classes. In the previous listing, we used method calls from the `ArrayList` class that you're familiar with from the review of lists in Chapter 3, but we could have used any method call that returned a valid data type.

Numeric Expressions

The first type of expressions, numeric, is perhaps the most familiar to the average person. We've seen countless formulas when we weren't paying attention in math class, and this is essentially how you write formulas in Java. Numeric expressions can be compound expressions and use numeric operators to connect multiple simple expressions together.

Listing 4-2. Examples of Numeric Expressions

```
01 //preparation
02 ArrayList<Integer> listIntegers;
03 listIntegers = new ArrayList();
04 listIntegers.add(10);
05
06 //simple numeric expressions
07 int i = 5;
08 i = 10;
09 i = 5 + 5;
10 i = 11 - 1;
11 i = 11 + -1;
12 i = 100 / 10;
13 i = 100 % 3;
14 i = (1 * 10);
15
16 i = 5;
17 i = i + 5;
18 i = i - +5;
19 i = i / 5;
20 i = i % 5;
21 i = (i * 5);
22
23 //compound numeric expressions
24 int j;
25 double d;
26 float f;
27 i = 0 + 10 - 5;
28 j = listIntegers.get(0) + 256;
29 s = "Hello" + " " + "World!";
30 d = 10 / 2.5 + 3;
31 d = 10 * 2.5 - 3;
32 f = (float)(12.7 / 10);
33 listIntegers.set(0, 125 + j + i);
```

A set of simple and compound numeric expressions.

Numeric expressions are used frequently in variable initialization and in flow control statements like If-Else statements. In the next section, we'll discuss the second most integral form of expressions in Java: the Boolean expressions.

Boolean Expressions

The second type of expressions we'll discuss is the Boolean expressions. Boolean expressions, both simple and compound, are shown in the previous listing, Listing 4-1. These are mainly used in the initialization of Boolean variables and If-Else statements.

Boolean expressions are an important part of just about every program as they are integral to the main flow control statement: the If-Else statement. We've seen a version of this before on line 71 with regard to the ternary operator that performs a function similar to an inline If-Else statement.

Listing 4-3. Examples of Boolean Expressions

```
01 //preparation
02 ArrayList<Integer> listIntegers;
03 listIntegers = new ArrayList();
04 listIntegers.add(10);
05
06 //simple boolean expressions
07 boolean b;
08 b = i == 5;
09 b = (j != d);
10 b = (j < d);
11 b = j > listIntegers.get(0);
12 b = (j <= i);
13 b = j >= d;
14
15 //compound boolean expressions
16 b = i + 1 == 5 + j;
17 b = (j + listIntegers.get(0) != d);
18 b = j < d + 100;
```

```
19 b = j / 2 > (listIntegers.get(0) * 2);
20 b = (j <= i++);
21 b = j >= -d;
```

A set of simple and compound Boolean expressions.

One more aspect of Boolean expressions I should mention is the concept of Boolean logic. It's beyond the scope of this text to cover Boolean logic, but you should spend some time reading up on it as it will greatly improve your use of Boolean operators in If-Else statements.

Assignment Expressions

The Java programming language has a full set of assignment expressions that combine numeric operators and assignments into one convenient step. For instance, the long form of the assignment expressions you'll see next is in Listing 4-4.

Listing 4-4. Long-Form Equivalent of Assignment Expressions

```
1 i = 5;
2 i = i + 5;
3 i = i - 5;
4 i = i / 5;
5 i = i % 5; //modulo operator returns the remainder of integer division
6 i = (i * 5);
```

A set of example long-form equivalent assignment expressions.

The short form of the previous expressions uses Java's convenient assignment operators.

Listing 4-5. Examples of Assignment Expressions

```
1 i = 5;
2 i += 5;
3 i -= 5;
4 i /= 5;
5 i %= 5;
6 i *= 5;
```

A set of example assignment expressions.

It may seem like overkill to have this level of specificity in our assignment operators, but use them a few times and you'll be hooked. In the next section, we'll take a look at some convenience operators that make incrementing and decrementing a value more efficient.

Increment/Decrement Expressions

The Java language has some shortcuts when it comes to the common practice of incrementing or decrementing a value. This happens so frequently in programming that there is literally a special operator just for it. First, let's take a look at the ways we can increment/decrement a variable using our current set of tools.

```
i = i + 1;
i += 1;
i = i - 1;
i -= 1;
```

To make things just that much easier, you also now have the following options available to you for incrementing and decrementing a variable by 1:

```
i++;
i--;
```

I should mention that you can also use the forms ++i and --i, which are only different in the sense that the order of operations is different. In one case, you have increment then assign; in the other case, you have assign then increment. Let's look at a subtle result of this distinction in Listing 4-6.

Listing 4-6. Examples of Assignment Expressions

```
//code
01 int q; //declare
02
03 q = 5; //init
04 int q1 = q++;
05
06 q = 5; //init
```

```
07 int q2 = ++q;
08
09 System.out.println("q++: " + q1);
10 System.out.println("++q: " + q2);
//output
01 q++: 5
02 ++q: 6
```

An example of the distinction between using ++q, --q and q++, q--.

Can you see the distinction in the example code in Listing 4-6? In one case, the value is assigned, and then it is incremented, line 4, while in the second case, the value is incremented and then assigned, line 7. The resulting output shows the difference in the assigned value. That's all I want to cover on this topic. In the next section, we'll take a look at the bitwise operations that you can perform on integer-based variables.

Bitwise Expressions

Bitwise expressions aren't used that often. In fact, you can probably program in Java for years without using them once. This is because they are rather low level and as such only come in handy when working with bytes and binary data. However, that's not an excuse not to have some level of familiarity with them, so let's take a look.

Listing 4-7. Examples of Bitwise Expressions

```
01 //preparation
02 int x, y, z;
03
04 //simple bitwise expressions
05 x = 5;
06 y = 7;
07 z = x | y; //bitwise OR, z = 7
08 z = x & y; //bitwise AND, z = 5
09 z = x ^ y; //bitwise XOR, z = 2
10 z = ~x; //bitwise compliment, z = 10
11
```

```
12 //compound bitwise expressions
13 z = ++x | y--;
14 z = x * y & y + 10;
15 z = x ^ y / 256;
16 z = ~(x * 2);
```

An example of simple and compound bitwise expressions.

To go over the bit-level operations is beyond the scope of this text. Take a moment to look up the Boolean operations AND, XOR, and OR and bitwise complement to learn more about them. Again, this is a somewhat erudite area of the Java programming language. It may be enough to have a passing familliarity with the material. In the next section, we'll take a look at some of the other bit-level expressions Java supports.

Bit-Shift Expressions

The last main set of expressions we'll discuss is also bit level; they are the bit-shift expressions. While you might think that these are useless to you as you will not be doing any binary programming, think again. Bit shifting is a very fast way to multiply or divide by 2.

This happens to be an adjustment that is made very frequently in certain situations and is worth being aware of. If you find yourself multiplying or dividing by 2 with any frequency, you might want to look into using a bit-shift operator. Let's take a quick look at some bit-shift expressions.

Listing 4-8. Example of Bit-Shift Expressions

```
//code
1 byte a = 64, g;
2 i = a << 2;
3 g = (byte)(a << 2);
4 System.out.println("a: " + a);
5 System.out.println("i and g: " + i + ", " + g);

//output
1 a: 64
2 i and g: 256, 0
```

An example of a simple bit-shift expression with comparison between integer and byte variable assignment of the shifted value.

Notice that in the previous listing, the original value 64 is now 256, which is 64 * 4. What does that tell us about the nature of shifting a value left two positions? Well, it tells us that a two-position bit shift to the left is the same as multiplying by 4. Similarly, a one position bit shift to the left is the same as multiplying by 2 and so on. In the reverse, when bit shifting to the right, we are dividing. For example, starting with a value of 256 and performing a two-position bit shift to the right divides 256 by 4, resulting in a value of 64, the original value.

The difference between the signed right shift, >>, and the unsigned right shift, >>>, is that with the signed shift, the bit values are pushed to the right and a new bit, with the same value as the number's sign, is added on the left of the number. With an unsigned shift, the new bit always has a value of zero.

Again, bit operations aren't for everyone, and if you don't need or want to use them, simply don't. But you should be aware the functionality exists even if you're not entirely comfortable using it. You can always look up some examples before you start coding. Next up we'll summarize the language's entire set of operators and sort them by precedence.

Operators and Operator Precedence

Now that we've covered all the main categories of expressions that Java supports, we should take a complete look at all of the operators involved and sort them by operator precedence. What is operator precedence? Operator precedence is the order in which the operators are processed as part of an expression.

The subsequent list shows Java operators from the most important, first processed, to the least important, last processed. Next to the text description of each operator is the symbol for it.

- Array index **[ ]**, member access **.**, method call **.**, post-decrement **--**, post-increment **++**

- Bitwise complement **~**, cast **( )**, logical complement **!**, object creation **new**, pre-decrement **--**, pre-increment **++**, unary minus **-**, unary plus **+**

- Division **/**, multiplication *****, remainder **%**

- Addition **+**, string concatenation **+**, subtraction **-**

- Left shift **<<**, signed right shift **>>**, unsigned right shift **>>>**

- Greater than **>**, greater than or equal to **>=**, less than **<**, less than or equal to **<=**, type checking **instanceof**

- Equality **==**, inequality **!=**

- Bitwise AND **&**, logical AND **&&**

- Bitwise exclusive OR **^**, logical exclusive OR **^ (on Boolean operators)**

- Bitwise inclusive OR **|**, logical inclusive OR **||**

- Conditional AND **&& (on Boolean operators)**

- Conditional OR **|| (on Boolean operators)**

- Conditional **?: (ternary operator)**

- Assignment **=**, compound assignment **+=, -+, *=, /=, %=, &=, ^=, /=, <<=, >>=, >>>=**

This isn't something you need to necessarily memorize, but it's something you should be aware of. In most cases, I would recommend using parenthesis to group the operators and values and control precedence explicitly. That brings us to the conclusion of this section. In the next section, we'll take a look at different ways that we can control the flow of a Java program.

Flow Control

While you've learned a considerable amount up to this point, we still only know how to declare variables and model our data. We don't have much in the way of controlling how the program executes. Flow control is an essential part of any program. Without it, we wouldn't be able to execute an alternate branch of code based on the value of a variable. You can't write many interesting programs without flow control.

We'll take a look at three different ways that you can control the flow of a Java program. The first is the traditional If-Else statement including the Else-If clause. The second is a statement that is used to support separating into many different branches of code: the Switch statement. Lastly, we have a method of flow control that allows us to alter the course of the program in response to exceptions, unexpected errors, in the program using Try-Catch statements. Let's take a look!

If-Else Statements

If-Else statements (this also includes the Else-If clause, but we'll exclude explicitly listing it for brevity) are the primary way you will control the flow of execution in a Java program. An If-Else statement takes a Boolean expression and conditionally executes certain code depending on the result of the expression. Boolean expressions of this type are referred to as conditionals. Let's take a look at a basic If-Else statement without an explicit condition expressed.

Listing 4-9. Example of Basic If-Else Statement

```
1 if(conditional expression) {
2     //then clause
3 } else {
4     //else clause
5 }
```

An example of a basic If-Else statement without an explicit conditional expression.

Let's further this concept with a simple example where we use an If-Else statement to control the initialization of a variable.

Listing 4-10. Example of If-Else Statement and Variable Initialization

```
1 boolean b = true;
2 int i = 0;
3 if(!b) {
4     //then clause
5     i = 5;
6 } else {
7     //else clause
8     i = 10;
9 }
```

An example of using an If-Else statement to control variable initialization.

Something about this use of the If-Else statement should seem familiar, no? Can you think of another way to do the same thing using something we already have in our toolbox? Here's a hint: it's also a form of conditional. If you thought about the ternary operator, then you thought right.

Listing 4-11. Example of If-Else Statement and Variable Initialization

```
1 boolean b = true;
2 int i = !b ? i = 5 : i = 10;
```

An example of using a conditional to do the same variable initialization as an If-Else statement.

Of course, there's more to it If-Else statements that just the basic form, and the initialization of variables. Let's look at an example from the Pong Clone game's ScreenGame.java class. You can find this Java class in the net.middlemind.PongClone package.

Listing 4-12. Example of Complex If-Else Statement from ScreenGame.java

```
01 public boolean ProcessKeyPress(char c, int code) {
02     if(state == State.SHOW_GAME && pause == false) {
03         if(gameType == GameType.GAME_TWO_PLAYER) {
04             if(c == 'x' || c == 'X') {
05                 paddle1MoveUp = false;
06                 paddle1MoveDown = true;
07                 return true;
08             } else if(c == 's' || c == 'S') {
09                 paddle1MoveUp = true;
10                 paddle1MoveDown = false;
11                 return true;
12             }
13         }
14     }
15     return false;
16 }
```

A complex example of the If-Else statement in use to process keyboard input for the Pong Clone game.

Let's focus on the If-Else statement on lines 4–13. We'll pull this If-Else statement out and adjust its structure a little bit.

Listing 4-13. Example of Expanded If-Else Statement

```
01 if(c == 'x') {
02     paddle1MoveUp = false;
03     paddle1MoveDown = true;
04     return true;
05 } else if(c == 'X') {
06     paddle1MoveUp = false;
07     paddle1MoveDown = true;
08     return true;
09 } else if(c == 's') {
10     paddle1MoveUp = true;
11     paddle1MoveDown = false;
12     return true;
13 } else if(c == 'S') {
14     paddle1MoveUp = true;
15     paddle1MoveDown = false;
16     return true;
17 }
```

An example of an expanded If-Else statement where each case has its own Else-If clause.

Notice that we can use If-Else statements, well technically If-Else-If statements but you get the idea, to check a bunch of different related conditions. The syntax is a bit redundant in that we have to check the value of the same variable over and over again, once for each branch. Think about this for a minute. This sounds like a common occurrence in programming. While, clearly, we can handle this using an If-Else statement, there's a slightly cleaner way to do it using a Switch statement.

Switch Statements

Switch statements are another flow control tool in the Java programming language, and they come in handy mainly when there are multiple, different, actions that must be taken based on the value of a certain variable. In the preceding example, that variable is the character variable c. Let's take a look at an equivalent snippet of code that replaces the If-Else statement with a Switch statement.

Listing 4-14. Example of Switch Statement

```
01 switch(c) {
02     case 'x':
03         paddle1MoveUp = false;
04         paddle1MoveDown = true;
05         return true;
06     case 'X':
07         paddle1MoveUp = false;
08         paddle1MoveDown = true;
09         return true;
10     case 's':
11         paddle1MoveUp = true;
12         paddle1MoveDown = false;
13         return true;
14     case 'S':
15         paddle1MoveUp = true;
16         paddle1MoveDown = false;
17         return true;
18 }
```

An example of a Switch statement where each case has replaced an If-Else or Else-If clause.

Take a moment to look over the Switch statement's structure. Each Else-If statement is replaced by a case statement entry that checks a specific value. Normally, a Switch statement's case clause is concluded with a break statement, but a return statement works just fine in certain circumstances. Let's take a look at a slightly re-structured Switch statement that more closely matches the first If-Else statement we looked at, and we'll replace the return statement with a break statement.

Listing 4-15. Example of Switch Statement with Break and Default Case

```
01 switch(c) {
02     case 'x':
03     case 'X':
```

```
04          paddle1MoveUp = false;
05          paddle1MoveDown = true;
06          break;
07      case 's':
08      case 'S':
09          paddle1MoveUp = true;
10          paddle1MoveDown = false;
11          break;
12      default:
13          paddle1MoveUp = false;
14          paddle1MoveDown = false;
15          break;
16 }
```

An example of a Switch statement where each case has replaced an Else-If clause.

As we mentioned earlier, this is a slightly adjusted Switch statement. Notice that the "x" and "X" conditions evaluate to the same case branch code. This is an example of using the Switch statement's case clause without an exit statement, break or return, to group up similar branches of code. For instance, the same code is run when the user presses the "x" key as when they have Caps Lock on and press "X". This is the same structure that's in the original If-Else statement we looked at earlier. Lastly, the Switch statement has a default case. This is similar to the Else clause of an If-Else-If statement. The default case executes in the case there isn't a direct match on a previous Switch statement case.

For the most part, Switch statements are really straightforward. They closely follow the logic of If-Else statements but provide a cleaner syntax in certain scenarios. Switch statements can only be used with certain data types – byte, short, char, int – and enumerated data types like arrays and enumerations. In the next section, we'll take a look at a different form of flow control: error handling with Try-Catch statements.

Try-Catch Statements

Up until this point, the flow control statements we've reviewed are explicit statements where we check the value of a variable and make a decision as to which branch of code to execute. The If-Else statement is very good at handling this in most cases. Every now and then you will need to use a Switch statement to take advantage of the cleaner syntax when comparing the same variable's value for multiple different branches of code.

There are some cases where you need to control the flow of the program but not in the normal scenarios we've looked at prior. In this circumstance, we're interested in controlling the flow of the program when an error occurs. For this particular situation, Java provides us with the Try-Catch statement. Let's take a look at a basic example.

Listing 4-16. Example of Try-Catch Statement

```
//code
1 try {
2     int t;
3     String u = "test";
4     t = Integer.parseInt(u);
5 } catch (Exception e) {
6     e.printStackTrace();
7 }

//output
1 java.lang.NumberFormatException: For input string: "test"
```

An example of a Try-Catch statement being used to control program flow around an error.

In the previous listing, on line 3, the initialization of the String u is incorrect. The variable is initialized to a word and not a number string. Normally, this would be a perfectly fine choice, but on line 4, we're using the string variable as the source value to convert to an Integer. Now, this code will fail and throw a NumberFormatException – that we can catch!

For our purposes, we're catching the more general, Exception. This is fine for our demonstration, but you should keep your Try-Catch statements aligned to the type of exceptions they are meant to handle. Now, in this example, all we do is report the error, line 6, but we could have taken any number of measures in the catch clause to correct the exception encountered or we could report the issue and gracefully exit the program.

In either case, we're able to control the flow of the program after encountering an exception because we employed the Try-Catch statement around code that could potentially be the source of an error, that is, throw an exception. In this way, we can make our own Java programs very stable by using Try-Catch statements to protect code that could generate an error while responding to the error accordingly.

That brings us to the conclusion of this section. In the next section, we'll reinforce our knowledge on program flow control with a challenge on the subject. Let's check out the challenge and jump into some code!

Challenge: Flow Control

In our first challenge for this chapter, we'll use our knowledge of flow control to alter a copy of the Pong Clone game. This challenge will require us to alter the game's input handling to support more keyboard keys. Let's take a look at the details.

Packages Involved:

```
net.middlemind.PongClone_Chapter4_Challenge1
net.middlemind.PongClone_Chapter4_Challenge1_Solved
```

Description:

Find the package, net.middlemind.PongClone_Chapter4_Challenge1, and open the ScreenGame.java file. Some of the testers are reporting that it's kind of difficult to control the paddles when playing a two-player game. We'll have to map two new sets of two keys each to add new paddle down and up controls for players 1 and 2.

Find the `ProcessKeyPress` and `ProcessKeyRelease` methods of the `ScreenGame` class. You'll have to use your knowledge of Java flow control statements to add support for two new sets of keyboard keys: one for player1 to move the paddle up and down and a set for player2 to do the same. Use the code that's already in place for player1 as a template. You must run this package's file – PongClone.java; right-click and select Run File to test the game.

Clue:

You'll have to set the following variables to true or false depending on the keyboard key used and if the key is being pressed or released:

- paddle1MoveUp

- paddle1MoveDown

- paddle2MoveUp

- paddle2MoveDown

Remember, you have to reset the Boolean variable in the key release method, `ProcessKeyRelease`; otherwise, the player's paddle will be stuck, moving either up or down.

In order to run the package's specific version of the game, you have to click on the static main class contained in that package and select "Run File" from the context menu. Otherwise, the project's default game will execute. If you've solved the challenge correctly, the game should run properly and allow you to control the player1 and player2 paddle using the new keyboard mappings you just made.

Challenge Solution

The solution to this challenge requires you to make two changes to the challenge package's ScreenGame.java file, specifically in the ProcessKeyPress and ProcessKeyRelease methods. The first part of the solution requires us to follow the example in the ProcessKeyPress method so that we can support new keys in the same way as the original control keys. Let's take a look at one example of a valid solution to this challenge.

Listing 4-17. A Possible Solution to Challenge 1

```
01 public boolean ProcessKeyPress(char c, int code) {
02      if(state == State.SHOW_GAME && pause == false) {
03          if(gameType == GameType.GAME_TWO_PLAYER) {
04              if(c == 'x' || c == 'X' || c == '1' || c == '!') {
05                  paddle1MoveUp = false;
06                  paddle1MoveDown = true;
07                  return true;
08
09              } else if(c == 's' || c == 'S' || c == '2' || c == '@') {
10                  paddle1MoveUp = true;
11                  paddle1MoveDown = false;
12                  return true;
13              }
14
15              if(c == '9' || c == '(') {
16                  paddle2MoveUp = false;
17                  paddle2MoveDown = true;
18                  return true;
19
```

```
20            } else if(c == 'o' || c == ')') {
21                    paddle2MoveUp = true;
22                    paddle2MoveDown = false;
23                    return true;
24                }
25            }
26        }
27    return false;
28 }
29
30 public boolean ProcessKeyRelease(char c, int code) {
31     if(state == State.SHOW_GAME && pause == false) {
32         if(gameType == GameType.GAME_TWO_PLAYER) {
33             if(c == 'x' || c == 'X' || c == '1' || c == '!') {
34                    paddle1MoveDown = false;
35                    return true;
36
37             } else if(c == 's' || c == 'S' || c == '2' || c == '@') {
38                    paddle1MoveUp = false;
39                    return true;
40                }
41
42             if(c == '9' || c == '(') {
43                    paddle2MoveDown = false;
44                    return true;
45
46             } else if(c == 'o' || c == ')') {
47                    paddle2MoveUp = false;
48                    return true;
49                }
50            }
51        }
52    return false;
53 }
```

An example of a possible solution to challenge 1.

One important thing that should stand out to you is the separation of the player1 and player2 key event handler into two different If-Else statements. Why do you think that is? Well, if you think about how we converted an If-Else statement into a Switch statement, what would happen if both player1 and player2 inputs were handled by the same Switch statement?

If you're thinking that both players would not be able to process key presses at the same time due to the nature of a Switch statement only processing one case clause, you'd be right. The same thing would happen if we only used one If-Else statement. If we want both players' input to function independently, we need to make the input handling code function independently by using two separate If-Else statements.

More on Variables

We covered a fair amount of material in this chapter so far, but I wanted to swing back around to the subject of variables and briefly discuss a few finer points to really round out our review of the subject. Now that we have experience working with different Java expressions and have explicitly covered Boolean expressions and If-Else statements, there are a few more things I want to cover on the subject of variables.

I would like to briefly explore the topics of custom data types and data type casting, conversion with regard to variables in Java. First up, we'll tackle custom data types with an introduction to Enumerations.

Enumerations

The Java programming language has the concept of an Enumeration. An Enumeration is a list of named constants. In Java, an Enumeration defines a class type. An Enumeration can have constructors, methods, and instance variables. It is created using the enum keyword. Each enumeration constant is public, static, and final by default.

The information on class features like constructors, methods, and field access, public or static, will be explained in more detail when we cover Java classes. You'll get some very basic exposure to classes in this chapter. For now, simply follow along and keep these concepts at the back of your mind. Don't fret if you don't quite understand them yet. Let's look at a basic, but common, use of the enum keyword to create an enumeration.

Listing 4-18. Example of Basic Enumeration Use

```
01 private enum State {
02     NONE,
03     SHOW_GAME,
04     SHOW_COUNT_DOWN,
05     SHOW_COUNT_DOWN_IN_GAME,
06     SHOW_GAME_OVER,
07     SHOW_GAME_EXIT
08 };
09
10 public State gameState = State.NONE;
```

An example of basic enumeration use including variable declaration and initialization.

Once you have an Enumeration declared and initialized, you can refer to its members using Java's member operator, ., like so:

```
if (gameState == State.SHOW_GAME) { ... }
```

This makes using enumerations clean and intuitive. You could accomplish the same thing in another way. Let's say you use a set of integers to do the job.

```
int NONE = -1;
int SHOW_GAME = 0;
int SHOW_COUNT_DOWN = 1;
int SHOW_COUNT_DOWN_IN_GAME = 2;
int SHOW_GAME_OVER = 3;
int SHOW_GAME_EXIT = 4;
```

This implementation is not so bad. It's intuitive and also clean. One issue though is that we have to explicitly define a unique value for the integers representing the different variables. Whereas prior, the enumeration took care of this for us. Let's see what this approach looks like in practice.

```
if (gameState == SHOW_GAME) { ... }
```

The difference is subtle, but in the prior example, we lose the concept of "State". This is slightly less important in the example because the variable we're using is properly named, gameState. Still, without too much investigation, we can see the use of enumerations makes the code a little cleaner and a little more intuitive. Enumerations are a very powerful tool in the Java programming language. Keep them in mind when you're coding up your next project.

Very Basic Java Classes

It's clear that while enumerations have their use and can be easily customized creating a new data type for you to use in your programs, they also have their limitation. For one thing, the members have to be integers. That limitation alone will make us look elsewhere for other approaches to data type customization. Following along the same thread of discovery, we come to another way to create custom data types: the plain old Java class.

Listing 4-19. Example of a Basic Java Class

```
1 public class GameData {
2     public State gameState = State.NONE;
3     public int numberOfPlayers = 1;
4     public boolean gameOver = false;
5     public String playerName = "AAA";
6 }
7
8 public GameData gameMetaData;
9 gameMetaData = new GameData();
```

An example of a custom data type defined through a Java class.

The code in the previous listing should look somewhat similar to that of Listing 4-18. What we have here is a very simple Java class that is designed to hold a few different pieces of information. We have referred to these as variables before, but in this context, we shall call them class fields or more generally class members.

Notice that we can now create variables of this data type as shown on lines 8–9. This is very similar to the way we used enumerations, but in this case, we are able to create classes that hold fields of different types including other classes and enumerations. This gives us a lot of power in the type of data we can model. Think about that for a moment.

That brings us to the conclusion of this section. In the next section, we'll focus more on variables of the basic data types and how they can be converted to/from other different basic data types.

Casting and Conversion

Casting and conversion as we're discussing it here will be limited to the conversion of the basic data types – byte, char, short, int, long, float, double, String, boolean – to and from other basic data types. String conversion is unique, so let's get that one out of the way first. The following code snippet shows how to convert a String value to the other basic data types. Let's have a look!

Listing 4-20. Example of Converting from a String to the Basic Data Types

```
01 //prep
02 String u;
03
04 //byte
05 u = "128";
06 try {
07     byte tB;
08     tB = Byte.parseByte(u);
09 } catch (Exception e) {
10     //error, exit the program
11     return;
12 }
13
14 //char
15 u = "c";
16 try {
17     char tC = u.toCharArray()[0];
18 } catch (Exception e) {
19     //error, exit the program
20     return;
21 }
22
```

```
23 //short
24 u = "1024";
25 try {
26     short tS;
27     tS = Short.parseShort(u);
28 } catch (Exception e) {
29     //error, exit the program
30     return;
31 }
32
33 //int
34 u = "10";
35 try {
36     int tI;
37     tI = Integer.parseInt(u);
38 } catch (Exception e) {
39     //error, exit the program
40     return;
41 }
42
43 //long
44 u = "2048";
45 try {
46     long tL;
47     tL = Long.parseLong(u);
48 } catch (Exception e) {
49     //error, exit the program
50     return;
51 }
52
53 //float
54 u = "100.05";
55 try {
56     float tF;
57     tF = Float.parseFloat(u);
58 } catch (Exception e) {
```

```
59    //error, exit the program
60    return;
61 }
62
63 //double
64 u = "200.10";
65 try {
66    double tD;
67    tD = Double.parseDouble(u);
68 } catch (Exception e) {
69    //error, exit the program
70    return;
71 }
72
73 //boolean
74 u = "true";
75 try {
76    boolean tBl;
77    tBl = Boolean.parseBoolean(u);
78 } catch (Exception e) {
79    //error, exit the program
80    return;
81 }
```

A block of code showing conversion between a String and other basic data types.

It looks a bit complicated, so we'll talk about what's going on here. Converting from a String data type to another basic data type isn't that straightforward. There's a bit of an encoding involved. For instance, if the string value that we're converting isn't a "true" or "false" value, then we won't be able to accurately convert it to a Boolean, and an exception will be thrown.

To perform the actual conversion, we rely on the "boxed" version of the data types – Byte, Short, Integer, Long, Float, Double, and Boolean. For the char conversion, we simply use the first character value in the string. This could be null or otherwise nonexistent, so we are prepared to catch an exception during this conversion as well. For the remaining basic data types, we use a parse method, which is a static method of the object version of the basic data types.

A static method is a method that is defined for the class itself, not an instance of the class. For instance, to convert a String, s, to an int, j, you would use the following method call:

```
j = Integer.parseInt(s);
```

And be prepared to catch an exception in case the string doesn't contain an integer in string form. Let's look at how we would convert from the other basic data types to the String data type.

Listing 4-21. Example of Converting from the Basic Data Types to a String

```
01 //prep
02 String u;
03
04 u = (tB + ""); //byte
05 u = (tC + ""); //char
06 u = (tS + ""); //short
07 u = (tI + ""); //int
08 u = (tL + ""); //long
09 u = (tF + ""); //float
10 u = (tD + ""); //double
11 u = (tBl + ""); //boolean
```

A null-safe way to convert from basic data type to the String data type. It continues from the code in Listing 4-20.

In Listing 4-21, which continues from the code in Listing 4-20, we can see a null-safe way to convert each of the basic data types to the String data type. What makes this a null-safe way to convert the variable's value? Notice that no method call is made to convert the values. Instead, we're relying on the Java language itself, which converts an Object; in this case, it automatically boxes the basic data type converting it to an object of type – Byte, Short, Integer, Long, Float, Double, Boolean. Then it calls the internal toString method returning a string that can then be concatenated with the empty string. In this way, we can return a string value without calling a method.

Now that we have got converting a String to and from the basic data types down, we can talk about converting some of the numeric basic data types to and from other numeric basic data types. It turns out that without any concern, we can convert from smaller data types to larger data types in some cases. For instance, the following conversions are allowed.

Listing 4-22. Example of Implicit and Explicit Variable Conversion

```
01 //implicit conversion
02 byte b = 8;
03 //char c = b; //cannot convert to char implicitly
04 int i = b;
05 long l = b;
06 float f = b;
07 double d = b;
08
09 //explicit conversion
10 f = (float)d;
11 l = (long)d;
12 i = (int)d;
13 c = (char)d;
14 b = (byte)d;
```

An example demonstrating the conversion of numeric basic data types to other numeric basic data types.

The implicit conversions are done automatically by the compiler without so much as a complaint. The reason is that we're converting from a smaller data type to a larger data type so there's no possibility of data loss, lines 1–7. When converting data types in the other direction, though, we'll get an error unless we tell the compiler that we're aware the conversion we're doing could possibly cause a loss of data. Why would data be lost?

Well, it's literally a matter of space. The amount of information used to describe a long could not fit into a byte. When converting from a long to a byte, we face the possibility of data loss because a byte can't hold numbers as large as a variable of data type long. In order to perform this type of conversion, we have to let the compiler know that we are aware of the danger. We do so by adding the destination data type surrounded by parenthesis in front of the assignment operator. Try applying explicit and implicit casting to variables of other basic data types.

Challenge: Enumerations

The second challenge for this chapter is a bit more complex than previous challenges, but don't worry, you can use existing code as a template for all the changes required to solve this challenge.

Packages Involved:

```
net.middlemind.PongClone_Chapter4_Challenge2
net.middlemind.PongClone_Chapter4_Challenge2_Solved
```

Description:

Find the package, net.middlemind.PongClone_Chapter4_Challenge2, and open the ScreenGame.java file. One of the lead programmers on the project wants to test making the countdown longer. Your challenge is to increase the countdown from three to five seconds. You'll also update the images used for the countdown so that they don't have the blue border. This will make our changes stand out a bit.

In order to accomplish this challenge, you have to do a few things. I'll list the general steps here.

1. Update the countdown enumeration to support numbers 4 and 5. Use the existing enumeration entries as a basis for your change.

2. Update the class to include variables number4 and number5. Use the existing variables – number1, number2, and number3 – as a basis for your change.

3. Locate the LoadResources method in the ScreenGame class and find where the variables number1, number2, and number3 are initialized. Add number4 and number5 to the variables initialized. Use the existing code as a basis for the new variables.

4. Change the files used to initialize the number 1–5 variables by adding a 2 before the ".png". For instance, the file name "num_1_lrg.png" becomes "num_1_lrg2.png."

5. Locate the DrawScreen method and uncomment the new code that draws five numbers during the countdown and comment out the old code that only supported drawing three numbers.

Once those steps are complete, you should be able to run the package's PongClone.java class and play the game. You'll notice a five-second countdown to start the game and in-between points. Also, none of the number images have a blue outline.

Clue:

The best clue to give you for this challenge is to look at the code that is already in place and use it as a template.

In order to run the package's specific version of the game, you have to click on the static main class contained in that package and select "Run File" from the context menu. Otherwise, the project's default game will execute. If you've solved the challenge correctly, the game should run properly and display a five-second countdown with no blue borders around the numbers. Make sure to take your time with this challenge. It's easy to make a mistake due to the similarity between variable names.

Challenge: Solution

The solution to this challenge requires you to make four changes to the ScreenGame.java file. The first change is to add the new entries in the state tracking enumeration for the countdown timer. There are already entries for numbers 1 through 3, so you just have to use the existing code as a template and add numbers 4 and 5.

The second change you must make is to add new MmgBmp variables, number4 and number5, to represent the 4th and the 5th second of the countdown. Again, in this case, you have code present for declaring variables numbers 1–3. Use the existing code as a template and create variables for numbers 4 and 5. Similarly, find where these variables are initialized in the LoadResources method and add in the necessary code for numbers 4 and 5.

This step can seem somewhat daunting, but if you give yourself some space, just paste in a copy of one of the existing code initialization snippets and customize it for numbers 4 and 5, respectively. I'll show an example of the snippet of code for initializing a number variable.

Listing 4-23. Example of the Initialization of a Number Variable

```
01 //Load number three config
02 key = "bmpNumberThree";
03 if(classConfig.containsKey(key)) {
04     file = classConfig.get(key).str;
05 } else {
06     file = "num_3_lrg2.png";
07 }
```

```
08
09 lval = MmgHelper.GetBasicCachedBmp(file);
10 number3 = lval;
11 if(number3 != null) {
12     MmgHelper.CenterHorAndVert(number3);
13     number3 = MmgHelper.ContainsKeyMmgBmpScaleAndPosition("numberThree",
       number3, classConfig, number3.GetPosition());
14     number3.SetIsVisible(false);
15     AddObj(number3);
16 }
```

An example demonstrating the initialization of a number variable.

Remember, you also have to adjust the names of the image resources used to load numbers 1–3. Use file names that end in "2.png". If everything goes to plan, then you should see clean numbers in the new five-second countdown timer.

Image 4-1. *Screenshot of the Pong Clone Game with Five-Second Countdown Timer*

A screenshot showing the modified countdown timer in action. No blue outlines and a five-second countdown.

That brings us to the end of the second challenge and the conclusion of the chapter. We'll take a look at the material we've covered and wrap things up in the remaining sections.

Conclusion

That brings us to the end of this chapter on expressions, operators, flow control, and variables. We covered a decent amount of material and expanded our coding toolbox to include some very useful tools like If-Else and Switch statements. We're going to continue our exploration of the Java language by introducing you to a few more very useful data structures in the next chapter. Before we say farewell to this chapter, let's take a look at what we covered here.

What We Covered

The Java language features we covered in this language are as follows:

- Numeric Expressions: We took a look at one of the main types of expressions and associated operators: the numeric expressions.

- Boolean Expressions: The next most important type of expression in Java is the Boolean expression, and it's used to create conditionals that, when combined with flow control statements, allow us to control the execution of our program.

- Assignment Expressions: We took a moment to look at the different assignment expressions including the convenience of compound assignment operators.

- Increment/Decrement Expressions: This is a small but important topic. We quickly covered the different ways you can accomplish incrementing and decrementing a variable including some very efficient increment/decrement operators.

- Bitwise Expressions: Bitwise expressions are used to perform bit-level logic on numeric information like AND, OR, and XOR operations.

- Bit-Shift Expressions: A second erudite section of Java expressions; the bit-shift expressions are used to quickly multiply or divide a value and can be a faster replacement for certain multiplication.

- Operator Precedence: We briefly outlined the full spectrum of operator precedence including bitwise and ternary operators in the listing.

- If, If-Else, If-Else-If Statements: Our first look at flow control statements introduced us to If-Else statements and branching code.

- Switch Statements: We learned a second way to branch code but one that is more suitable for multiple branches of code based on a single variable.

- Try-Catch Statements: We learned a form of flow control that is triggered by an exception being thrown.

- Challenge: Flow Control: We took on an interesting challenge that asked us to create new key mappings in the Pong Clone game allowing player1 and player2 to control their paddles using the new keys.

- Enumerations: As part of our review of Java variables, we swung back around after the review on flow control and took a look at how to create custom data types through the use of enumerations.

- Very Basic Java Classes: The second technique we reviewed when creating custom data types in Java is by using very simple classes. We took a look at an example of a new, custom, data type that stored information about an executing game.

- Challenge: Enumerations: The last challenge of the chapter asked us to expand the current countdown timer implementation and add two seconds to it by supporting enumeration entries for numbers 4 and 5. We also had to adjust some class variables, their initialization, and the DrawScreen method's code to complete the challenge.

We have a decent set of tools to work with now. Not only can we use all the basic data types to write a solution in Java, we can also use flow control statements, casting, conversion, and custom data types, among other things. We'll pick up even more experience and knowledge as we look at some of the more advanced features that Java has to offer in the coming chapters!

CHAPTER 5

More Data Structures

Welcome to Chapter 5! In this chapter, we'll spend some more time exploring some common data structures provided by the Java programming language. A brief summary of the data structures we'll cover in this chapter is as follows:

- Multidimensional Arrays: Similar to the arrays you worked with prior to this chapter, just with more dimensions, allowing us to map tabular data, etc.

- Hashes: A very useful data structure that can be thought of as a dictionary. Hashes store key-value pairs. Hashes are sometimes referred to by their actual Java class name, Hashtable, or the colloquial term, dictionary.

- Stacks: An important data structure that allows push and pop access to a stack of values. These are the first data structures we've seen that remove their elements when they are accessed. They also have the property that they return the element for you with a method call.

- Queues: Last but not least, the queue is a data structure you should be familiar with if you've ever had to wait in line for something. A queue provides add or remove access to a list of values.

Java Programming Note: *All the data structures used in the text are either core features of the Java programming language or are contained in the java.util package. Add the line **import java.util.* to use these classes in your programs.*

Recall from our review in Chapter 3 that data structures are more advanced data types that hold other variables. Normally, data structures would be considered outside the scope of an introductory programming language text, but I feel that a gentle

© Victor G. Brusca 2023
V. G. Brusca, *Introduction to Java Through Game Development*, https://doi.org/10.1007/978-1-4842-8951-8_5

introduction to them will help you greatly when you further explore the topic. We've had some experience working with arrays and lists in Java, so we'll start the discussion with multidimensional arrays. You'll find the syntax and usage familiar. Let's take a look!

Multidimensional Arrays

Multidimensional arrays are an array of arrays. Let's think of arrays in Java as a row in a spreadsheet. Each column in the row represents an array index and holds some data. Now, with regard to a multidimensional array of two dimensions, let's think of this as an entire spreadsheet of rows and columns. One index into the array will specify the row to find the data, while the second index will define the column.

Declaring Multidimensional Arrays

The process for declaring multidimensional arrays should be familiar to you from your previous review of Java arrays. Let's take a look.

Listing 5-1. Multidimensional Array – Declaration Examples

```
1 int[] oneDimension = new int[10];
2 int[][] twoDimensions = new int[10][10];
3 int[][][] threeDimensions = new int[10][10][10];
```

An example demonstrating the declaration of arrays of 1, 2, or 3 dimensions.

Let's talk a little bit about what's going on in this example. The first line shows the declaration of a one-dimensional array, as you well know. The second line shows the declaration of a two-dimensional array. Note that a new set of brackets, [ ], is added for each new array index.

**Java Programming Note: *Be careful when using multidimensional arrays as you can eat up quite a bit of memory rather quickly. For instance, a three-dimensional array with 1000 elements in each array has 1 billion entries, not a paltry amount by any means.*

Using Multidimensional Arrays

Now that we understand how to declare multidimensional arrays, let's take a look at a few use cases for getting and setting array values.

Listing 5-2. Multidimensional Array – Use Case Examples 1

```
01 int[] dim1 = new int[10];
02 int[][] dim2 = new int[10][10];
03 int[][][] dim3 = new int[10][10][10];
04
05 //simple array index set
06 dim1[0] = 10;
07
08 //2-dimensional array index set
09 dim2[0] = new int[10];
10 dim2[0][0] = 11;
11
12 //3-dimensional array index set
13 dim3[0] = new int[10];
14 dim3[0][0] = new int[10];
15 dim3[0][0][0] = 12;
```

An example demonstrating setting a value using arrays of different dimensions.

Take a moment to look over the get/set code for multidimensional arrays in Listing 5-2. Notice that as the dimension of the array increases, we have more initialization to perform. We must initialize each dimension of the array explicitly before we can use those array indexes to get or set a value. In the subsequent listing, we'll take a look at how to get values out of a multidimensional array.

Listing 5-3. Multidimensional Array – Use Case Examples 2

```
//code
01 int[] dim1 = new int[10];
02 int[][] dim2 = new int[10][10];
03 int[][][] dim3 = new int[10][10][10];
04
```

```
05 //simple array index set
06 dim1[0] = 10;
07
08 //2-dimensional array index set
09 dim2[0] = new int[10];
10 dim2[0][0] = 11;
11
12 //3-dimensional array index set
13 dim3[0] = new int[10];
14 dim3[0][0] = new int[10];
15 dim3[0][0][0] = 12;
16
17 System.out.println("Dim1 Index: 0 Value: " + dim1[0]);
18 System.out.println("Dim2 Index: 0 Value: " + dim2[0]);
19 System.out.println("Dim2 Index: 0,0 Value: " + dim2[0][0]);
20 System.out.println("Dim3 Index: 0 Value: " + dim3[0]);
21 System.out.println("Dim3 Index: 0,0 Value: " + dim3[0][0]);
22 System.out.println("Dim3 Index: 0,0,0 Value: " + dim3[0][0][0]);

//output
01 Dim1 Index: 0 Value: 10
02 Dim2 Index: 0 Value: [I@50f8360d
03 Dim2 Index: 0,0 Value: 11
04 Dim3 Index: 0 Value: [[I@13c78c0b
05 Dim3 Index: 0,0 Value: [I@12843fce
06 Dim3 Index: 0,0,0 Value: 12
```

An example demonstrating getting a value from arrays of different dimensions.

Listing 5-3 adds some output to the previous listing so we can get an idea of how to get values from a multidimensional array. If you draw your attention to lines 1–6 of the output section, you'll see the values stored in the specified array at the specified index. Wait a minute, what are all those funny values in the output? Care to venture a guess? Well, before I go ahead and answer, look back to the initialization code and see what is being assigned to that array index.

If you thought that the strange looking values in the output, "[I@50f8360d," are a representation of the array value at that index, then you'd be right. Those are a form of memory location in the Java virtual machine and indicate to us that an object of some kind is stored in that array index. In a similar fashion, take a moment to look at the array indices that actually print out a value. Can you spot the distinction between the two? In one case, we're getting a value from an array index that holds an entire other array. In the other case, we're getting a value from an array element at the specified multidimensional index that specifies a basic data type value.

Let's take a quick look at how you can clear out and delete a multidimensional array in Listing 5-4.

Listing 5-4. Multidimensional Array – Deletion

```
01 int[] dim1 = new int[10];
02 int[][] dim2 = new int[10][10];
03 int[][][] dim3 = new int[10][10][10];
04
05 //simple array index set
06 dim1[0] = 10;
07
08 //2-dimensional array index set
09 dim2[0] = new int[10];
10 dim2[0][0] = 11;
11
12 //3-dimensional array index set
13 dim3[0] = new int[10];
14 dim3[0][0] = new int[10];
15 dim3[0][0][0] = 12;
16
17 //zero a simple array index value
18 dim1[0] = 0;
19
20 //delete the array
21 dim1 = null;
22
23 //zero a multi-dimensional array index value
24 dim2[0][0] = 0;
25
26 //delete the array at the specified index
```

```
27 dim2[0] = null;
28
29 //zero a multi-dimensional array index value
30 dim3[0][0][0] = 0;
31
32 //delete the array at the specified index
33 dim3[0][0] = null;
34
35 //delete the array at the specified index
36 dim3[0] = null;
37
38 //delete all arrays
39 dim1 = null;
40 dim2 = null;
41 dim3 = null;
```

An example demonstrating zeroing an array index value and deleting multidimensional arrays.

It should be enough to simply set the array variable to null to properly delete an array. However, if you have an array of objects (references are important in this case), then you may want to delete individual parts of a multidimensional array. In the previous listing, Listing 5-4, example code demonstrates how to delete different parts of a multidimensional array.

You might have noticed that the array indices that are set to null to clear a row or column of a multidimensional array are the same indices that required us to initialize a new instance of an array. Multidimensional arrays are a new powerful data structure we've added to our coding toolbox. We'll continue on this thread of discussion, as promised, and take a look at another very useful data structure Java has to offer: hashes.

Hashes

Hashing is the process of employing a function to map a key to a value storing the data in a hash table. Hashes are another important data type that functions much like a dictionary. Let's explore that idea for a moment. Can you think of a data structure we've learned about that almost acts like a dictionary? Think about arrays for a moment. What do you use to look up a value in an array? You use an index value that is an integer to find the data stored in that array index.

That sort of sounds like we're using a dictionary to look up a word except we're using numbers instead of words. As it turns out, you can use an array to implement a hash, but that's a little outside of the scope of this text. Java, as it so happens, has a very convenient implementation of the hash data structure called the Hashtable.

Declaring Hashtables

Hashes are a powerful tool to add to our coding toolbox. Now that we've had a brief introduction to the concept of hashes, let's take a look at how we can use them in the Java programming language. Let's have a look at how we declare and instantiate a hash table in Java.

Listing 5-5. Hashtables – Declaration Examples

```
1 //simple hashtable declaration, using default key, value data type as
  Object implicitly
2 Hashtable ht1 = new Hashtable();
3
4 //advanced hashtable declaration specifying key, value data type as
  Object explicitly
5 Hashtable<Object, Object> ht2 = new Hashtable<Object, Object>();
6
7 //advanced hashtable declaration specifying key, value data types as
  Integers and short form of initialization
8 Hashtable<Integer, Integer> ht3 = new Hashtable<>();
```

An example of declaring different hash tables using implicit and explicit data type specifications for the key and value pair.

At first glance, this might seem a bit complex. Let's talk through it and see what's going on. A quick thought before we continue, let's remember that the data structures we're looking at here are more advanced than basic data types and even some of the data structures we've reviewed earlier. When we define a Hashtable, we are setting up a mapping between keys and values.

That means given some key, you can look up a value. But both the key and value, in this case, also have their own data types. For instance, you could use a String for both and your Hashtable would function exactly like a little dictionary. Let me further the concept with an example.

Listing 5-6. Hashtables – String Key, Value Data Types

```
//code
1 String key = "Java";
2 String value = "Java is a computer programming language.";
3 Hashtable<String, String> ht = new Hashtable<>();
4
5 ht.put(key, value);
6 System.out.println("The value for key: " + key + " is: '" +
ht.get("Java") + "'");

//output
1 The value for key: Java is: 'Java is a computer programming language.'
```

An example of declaring a Hashtable, initializing it and setting, and getting a value.

Take a look at Listing 5-6. Notice the use of basic data type, String, in the key and value pair definition, <String, String>, when declaring the hash table. We've seen these angled brackets before when we reviewed ArrayLists. They are used to configure certain data structures by setting their internal data types. In this case, they are used to set the data type of the Hashtable's key and value.

Diverting our attention back to Listing 5-5, take a look at line number 2. Notice that we didn't specify a data type for the key or value of the hash table. No worries, Java takes care of it for us and will simply use a default data type, the Object data type. The Object data type is the parent of all classes defined in the Java programming language, even the ones you haven't created yet. We'll cover more on Objects when we cover object-oriented programming.

For now, it's safe to think of them as a placeholder for a less generic Object defined by you. For instance, you could choose to use a String object, like we did in Listing 5-6. On line 4 of Listing 5-5, we've used a form of Hashtable declaration that explicitly defines the data type of the key and value used by the hash table. Notice that we've explicitly defined the same data types that would have been used by default.

Next, on line 8 of Listing 5-5, we have a `Hashtable` declared with boxed basic data types, `Integers` as opposed to `ints`, for the table's keys and values. Don't worry if it's a bit confusing right now. We'll look at using hash tables next, and this will help refine your understanding of the data structure.

Using Hashtables

In this section, we'll take our new coding tool, `Hashtables`, for a spin and investigate some use cases like getting/setting values, clearing, and deleting `Hashtables`. Let's build on the example from Listing 5-6. Remember, when reading through these code samples, the data types of the key and value pair can be configured.

Try to focus on the use of the `Hashtable` itself and how methods are used to manipulate data in the table. We've seen how to declare and initialize `Hashtable` in the previous section. Next, let's take a look at how we can get/set values in a `Hashtable`.

Listing 5-7. Hashtables – Getting and Setting Values

```
//code
01 //prepare
02 String key = "Java";
03 String value = "Java is a computer programming language.";
04 Hashtable<String, String> ht = new Hashtable<>();
05
06 //set
07 ht.put(key, value);
08 ht.put("JRE", "Java Runtime Environment");
09 ht.put("JDK", "Java Development Kit");
10
11 //get
12 System.out.println("The value for key: " + key + " is: '" +
ht.get("Java") + "'");
13 System.out.println("The value for key: JRE is: '" +
ht.get("JRE") + "'");
14 key = "JDK";
15 System.out.println("The value for key: JDK is: '" + ht.get(key) + "'");
```

```
//output
01 The value for key: Java is: 'Java is a computer programming language.'
02 The value for key: JRE is: 'Java Runtime Environment'
03 The value for key: JDK is: 'Java Development Kit'
```

An example of setting and getting values in a Hashtable using variables and constants as keys and values.

Notice that we can use variables to specify the key and value pair of a Hashtable's put method as shown on line 7 of the listing. In this case, because we're working with Strings as our key and value data type, we can also explicitly set the value we want to store by using String constants.

Subsequently, on lines 12–15, we use the Hashtable's get method to pull values from the data structure and append them to our output message. Next up, let's take a look at how we can clear out a Hashtable's values. There are a few ways we can do this. Let's jump into some code!

Listing 5-8. Hashtables – Clearing Values Part 1

```
01 //prepare
02 String key = "Java";
03 String value = "Java is a computer programming language.";
04 Hashtable<String, String> ht = new Hashtable<>();
05
06 //set
07 ht.put(key, value);
08 ht.put("JRE", "Java Runtime Environment");
09 ht.put("JDK", "Java Development Kit");
10
11 //explicitly remove all entries
12 ht.remove(key);
13 ht.remove("JRE");
14 ht.remove("JDK");
15
16 //implicitly remove all entries
17 ht.clear();
```

An example of clearing values from a Hashtable using explicit and implicit approaches.

As you can see from the listing, in most cases, you'll want to know the key that you used to store your data. Without them, you could always clear the entire data structure, as shown on line 17, but what if you want to remove a specific entry and you don't have the key for it? Turns out there is a nifty little way to get all the keys stored in the hash table and store them in an ArrayList; recall from our review of ArrayLists in Chapter 3. Let's take a look at this approach next.

Listing 5-9. Hashtables – Clearing Values Part 2

```
//code
01 //prepare
02 String key = "Java";
03 String value = "Java is a computer programming language.";
04 Hashtable<String, String> ht = new Hashtable<>();
05
06 //set
07 ht.put(key, value);
08 ht.put("JRE", "Java Runtime Environment");
09 ht.put("JDK", "Java Development Kit");
10
11 ArrayList<String> keys = (ArrayList<String>)ht.keys();
12 for(String name : keys) {
13     ht.remove(name);
14 }
```

An example of clearing values from a Hashtable using an ArrayList as an enumeration.

The first few lines of code in Listing 5-9 are the same as the prior listing. The differences start on line 11. Notice that we're calling the Hashtable class' keys method that returns a value that we can cast as an ArrayList. Because the hash table's data type for its keys is a String, we need an ArrayList of Strings to store the information.

CHAPTER 5   MORE DATA STRUCTURES

As we've seen before, angled brackets, <>, in the list declaration are used to specify its data type. Our list can hold the keys from the hash table, and in doing so, we can iterate over the keys and access each value stored in the hash table. Keep in mind we don't have to have any knowledge of what's inside the hash table; we can now, in a data-driven way, iterate through and see what value each key is mapped to.

Notice in the example on line 13 that we specifically remove each entry from the hash table using this approach. With more advanced data structures, there's usually a lot more to talk about, and hash tables are no exception. For our purposes here, you have a solid foundation to build on and a powerful new tool in our coding toolbox. In the next section, we'll take a look at another data structure: the stack.

Stacks

Stacks are another fundamental data structure that is very useful in programming. It comes up frequently in different situations and in different algorithms. A stack is a bit more of an abstract data structure. It's based on the concept that the last item pushed into the stack is the first item popped out of it.

The reason why I would describe this data structure as abstract is that it can easily be implemented using some of the other data structures we've reviewed thus far. For instance, we could use an array or a list to implement a stack fairly easily. This is something to keep in mind when working with data structures because the way they are implemented can impact their performance in different ways.

**Game Programming Note: Not all data structures are created equally. They each have different attributes regarding their performance during common operations like retrieval, search, sort, etc. Take the time to choose the best data structure for your use case.

In the next section, we'll take a look at how to declare and initialize a stack in Java. We won't get into the underlying implementation of the stack, but we'll learn the basics of how to use one. Let's take a look!

Declaring Stacks

Java, being a mature and complete programming language, has an implementation of a stack already for us to use: the Stack class. In Listing 5-10, we'll take a look at how to declare and initialize one.

Listing 5-10. Stacks – Declaring Stacks

```
1 //basic stack declaration using the default data type, Object
2 Stack stck1;
3
4 //stack declaration using the String data type
5 Stack<String> stck2;
6
7 //stack declaration using the Object data type
8 Stack<Object> stck3;
```

An example of declaring a stack configured to hold different data types.

Simple enough, declaring a stack looks a lot like working with the other data structures we've reviewed thus far. Let's further the discussion with an example showing us how to instantiate a stack in different ways.

Listing 5-11. Stacks – Instantiating Stacks

```
01 //basic stack instantiation using the default data type, Object
02 Stack stck1;
03 stck1 = new Stack();
04
05 //stack instantiation using the String data type
06 Stack<String> stck2 = new Stack<String>();
07
08 //stack instantiation using the Object data type
09 Stack<Object> stck3;
10 stck3 = new Stack<>();
```

An example of instantiating a stack configured to hold different data types.

Declaring a stack is very similar to the other data structure declarations we've reviewed throughout the text. Take note of the use of angled brackets to customize the stack's data type. A shortcut is to use only the brackets, <>, excluding the data type when instantiating the variable. It is enough in Java to specify the data type in the declaration of the variable carrying that through to the instantiation is not mandatory. An example of this can be seen in the previous listing on lines 9–10. Now that we know how to declare a Stack, let's take a look at how we can use them.

Using Stacks

Stacks, as mentioned previously, have a specific property such that the first item pushed into the stack is always the last item removed from the stack. Let's start off the exploration by taking a look at how we initialize a stack. In the example in Listing 5-12, we'll look at an example using a stack configured to use Integers. Let's take a look at some code!

Listing 5-12. Stacks – Initializing Stacks

```
01 //prep
02 Stack<Integer> stck;
03 stck = new Stack<>();
04
05 //initialize
06 stck.push(0); //example of automatic boxing of int
07 stck.push(new Integer(1));
08 stck.push(Integer.valueOf(2));
09 stck.push(3);
10 stck.push(4);
```

An example of declaring and initializing a stack configured to hold Integers. Notice the automatic boxing of an int value on line 6.

When working with stacks, when we want to add a new piece of data into the Stack, we "push" it onto the stack. You'll notice in the previous listing that although the stack was configured to hold Integers, we got away with using just an int, line 6. This is because Java will automatically take care of converting the basic data type, int, to an object form, an Integer.

After initializing the stack, we have the following list of data elements at the following positions in the stack:

- Position: 4 Value: 0
- Position: 3 Value: 1
- Position: 2 Value: 2
- Position: 1 Value: 3
- Position: 0 Value: 4

This seems slightly counterintuitive since we added the 0 value to the stack first. If we were working with a list, the last element in the list would have a value of 4, because it was added first, not a value of 0. This has to do with the nature of a Stack; by design, it returns values using a first in, last out approach. By extension of this idea, the last value in would be the first value out.

As it turns out, that's exactly what we get. Let's further this discussion with an example demonstrating the get/set use case. Pay special attention to the order of the values returned. I will use simple, increasing values as data to make things that much clearer.

Listing 5-13. Stacks – Getting/Setting Values Part 1

```
//code
01 int val = 0;
02 stck.push(val);
03 System.out.println("Push #1 Value: " + val);
04
05 val = new Integer(1);
06 stck.push(val);
07 System.out.println("Push #2 Value: " + val);
08
09 val = Integer.valueOf(2);
10 stck.push(val);
11 System.out.println("Push #3 Value: " + val);
12
13 val = 3;
14 stck.push(val);
```

```
15 System.out.println("Push #4 Value: " + val);
16
17 val = 4;
18 stck.push(val);
19 System.out.println("Push #5 Value: " + val);
20
21 System.out.println("Pop #1 Value: " + stck.pop());
22 System.out.println("Pop #2 Value: " + stck.pop());
23 System.out.println("Pop #3 Value: " + stck.pop());
24 System.out.println("Pop #4 Value: " + stck.pop());
25 System.out.println("Pop #5 Value: " + stck.pop());

//output
01 Push #1 Value: 0
02 Push #2 Value: 1
03 Push #3 Value: 2
04 Push #4 Value: 3
05 Push #5 Value: 4
06 Pop #1 Value: 4
07 Pop #2 Value: 3
08 Pop #3 Value: 2
09 Pop #4 Value: 1
10 Pop #5 Value: 0
```

An example of declaring and initializing a stack configured to hold Integers followed by a demonstration of getting and setting stack values.

**Java Programming Note: Although you've seen a few different ways you can convert to/from boxed versions of the basic data types, boxed meaning Integer instead of int, Float instead of float etc. You should only do this manually if you must. Java will do it for you in most cases.

Putting it all together in one place really makes the pattern emerge, doesn't it? There are a lot of uses of this pattern in programming; recursion is one of them. Keep in mind that popping a value off of the stack removes it from the stack. If you want to iterate over the same stack multiple times, you must store and re-push the popped-off values. Can you think of a really simple use of the properties of the stack? Take a look at the next listing for an answer.

Listing 5-14. Stacks – Getting/Setting Values Part 2

```
01 Stack<Character> stck4 = new Stack<>();
02 char c = '!';
03
04 stck4.push(c);
05 System.out.println("Push #1 Value: " + c);
06
07 c = 'k';
08 stck4.push(c);
09 System.out.println("Push #2 Value: " + c);
10
11 c = 'c';
12 stck4.push(c);
13 System.out.println("Push #3 Value: " + c);
14
15 c = 'a';
16 stck4.push(c);
17 System.out.println("Push #4 Value: " + c);
18
19 c = 'B';
20 stck4.push(c);
21 System.out.println("Push #5 Value: " + c);
22
23 System.out.println("Pop #1 Value: " + stck4.pop());
24 System.out.println("Pop #2 Value: " + stck4.pop());
25 System.out.println("Pop #3 Value: " + stck4.pop());
26 System.out.println("Pop #4 Value: " + stck4.pop());
27 System.out.println("Pop #5 Value: " + stck4.pop());
//output
01 Push #1 Value: !
02 Push #2 Value: k
```

```
03 Push #3 Value: c
04 Push #4 Value: a
05 Push #5 Value: B
06 Pop #1 Value: B
07 Pop #2 Value: a
08 Pop #3 Value: c
09 Pop #4 Value: k
10 Pop #5 Value: !
```

In this example, we've used the properties of the Stack data structure to reverse a word.

In Listing 5-14, we can see a quick and dirty use of the Stack data structure. It's not the most interesting piece of code, but it will actually reverse words, so why not? As you can see, using a Stack has inherent properties that you should keep in mind when you're coding. This is an important tool in any programmer's toolbox but not one that gets as much use, still it is important to have a working familiarity with the stack. In the next section, we'll take a quick look at our next data structure: the Queue.

Queues

Queues are very similar to Stacks in many ways; as such, we won't have as detailed a discussion about them. Instead, we'll talk briefly about the difference between Stacks and Queues and reinforce our review with an example.

A Queue is similar to a Stack except it operates using a first in, first out method. Much like Stacks, Queues are abstract data structures, meaning they can be implemented using other data structures. They have the same type of interaction, namely, calling a method to add a value to the data structure and calling a method to pull a value from it.

Without further ado, let us motivate the discussion with an example. We're going to look at the code from Listing 5-14.

Listing 5-15. Queues – Example of Queue Refactored from Listing 5-14

```
//code
01 LinkedList<Character> ll = new LinkedList<>();
02 char c = '!';
03
04 ll.add(c);
```

```
05 System.out.println("Add #1 Value: " + c);
06
07 c = 'k';
08 ll.add(c);
09 System.out.println("Add #2 Value: " + c);
10
11 c = 'c';
12 ll.add(c);
13 System.out.println("Add #3 Value: " + c);
14
15 c = 'a';
16 ll.add(c);
17 System.out.println("Add #4 Value: " + c);
18
19 c = 'B';
20 ll.add(c);
21 System.out.println("Add #5 Value: " + c);
22
23 System.out.println("Poll #1 Value: " + ll.poll());
24 System.out.println("Poll #2 Value: " + ll.poll());
25 System.out.println("Poll #3 Value: " + ll.poll());
26 System.out.println("Poll #4 Value: " + ll.poll());
27 System.out.println("Poll #5 Value: " + ll.poll());

//output
01 Add #1 Value: !
02 Add #2 Value: k
03 Add #3 Value: c
04 Add #4 Value: a
05 Add #5 Value: B
06 Poll #1 Value: !
07 Poll #2 Value: k
08 Poll #3 Value: c
09 Poll #4 Value: a
10 Poll #5 Value: B
```

Compare the output of this listing with that of Listing 5-14. Can you see the difference between first in, last out and first in, first out?

As you can see from the output of Listing 5-15, the Queue behaves much like a line at the bathroom; the first person in line is the first person to leave the line and use the restroom. You must also remember that just like a queue for the bathroom, when someone leaves the line, they leave the queue. When you pull data out of a queue, it is removed from the queue.

That wraps up round two of our introduction to Java data structures! Well not quite, I wanted to spend a little bit of time talking about those angled brackets we use to configure the data type(s) our data structures use.

Parameterized Types and Data Structures

We've encountered them a number of times throughout our review of different data structures. They are the angled brackets, <>, we use to configure the given data structure's internal data types. Why do we need to do this you ask? Well let's think about this for a moment.

Although you haven't had a formal review on Java classes, you have had some exposure to them so far. In the Java programming language, the Object is the super-class of all other classes in Java. This means that the Object class is the most general of all the classes, and a variable of the Object data type can store an instance of a String, Integer, ArrayList, and any other class.

That sounds powerful. But it also sounds a little insecure. That means that if you don't specify a data type for your data structure, and the default data type, Object, is used, then any object can be stored in that data structure. That's just not good coding. It's error prone because you don't know what object you can expect from the data structure.

This puts the responsibility on the programmer, not the compiler, to make sure you use the data structure consistently. I don't know about you, but I'd rather rely on the compiler. By defining a specific data type to use with a given data structure, the compiler will ensure no variables of another data type are stored in that data structure, giving you one less thing to worry about.

Challenge: Stacks

This challenge is a bit more difficult than previous challenges because you have to not only adjust a variable's data type but also refactor its use by tracking down and replacing method calls from the ArrayList class with method calls from the Stack class. You also have to be aware of the caveat that iterating over a Stack removes the elements from it.

You have seen both data structures in use in a few examples from Chapters 3 and 5, so you have the tools to do the job. If you get stuck, re-read the challenge description and the clue.

Packages Involved:

```
net.middlemind.MemoryMatch_Chapter5_Challenge1
net.middlemind.MemoryMatch_Chapter5_Challenge1_Solved
```

Description:

Find the package, net.middlemind.MemoryMatch_Chapter5_Challenge1, and open the ScreenGame.java file. The data structure used to track clicked cards is an ArrayList. Some of the game programmers wanted to see how it would look to use a Stack instead. Refactor the code in the ScreenGame.java class to use a Stack as requested. You'll need to adjust code in a few places throughout the file. The variable used to track the clicked cards is called clickedCards.

Keep in mind when using the pop method, the value that was stored in the Stack is removed. This means that you'll have to keep track of popped values and restore them if you want to loop over a Stack multiple times. You can keep the MemoryItems popped off of the stack in another data structure and add them back in using the Stack class' addAll method. You must run this package's file – MemoryMatch.java; right-click and select Run File to test the game. Good luck!

Clue:

There are a few ways to find all the places in the file where you have to adjust some code. One way is to change the data type of the variable and look for the errors caused by this change. You could also perform a text search on the name of the variable or right-click the variable and select the "Find Usages" option. You'll have to change the class methods used to get/set values in the data structure from those used by an ArrayList to those used by a Stack. You'll have to create a new Boolean class field to track when a match has been found so you can decide if you need to add the elements popped off of the Stack back in.

Challenge Solution

The solution to this challenge is fairly straightforward but requires you to search through the file to find the locations where you have to change an ArrayList method, or constructor, to an equivalent method, or constructor, in the Stack class. Looking at the solution package will show you the exact locations of the changes you need to make.

The idea is to change these method calls:

```
clickedCards.add(itm);
clickedCards.get(i);
```

with:

```
clickedCards.push(itm);
clickedCards.pop();
```

You'll also need change the declaration and initialization of the variable. And you'll also have to make sure you don't lose data when popping values off of the stack. After you finish making the changes, run the local package version of the MemoryMatch.java file by right-clicking it and selecting the "Run File" option. You should see no disruption in the functionality of the game as the Stack will functionally replace the ArrayList in this case.

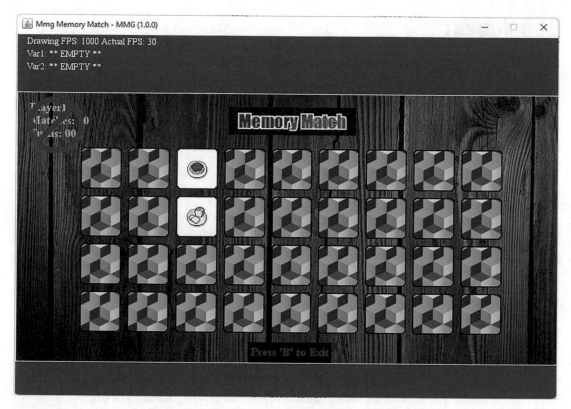

Image 5-1. *MemoryMatch with Stack-Based Click Tracking*

A screenshot showing the refactored code managing the clicked cards.

If you run into an error where only one of your cards resets, you need to look at the CheckForMatches method and make sure you are storing the popped elements and returning them to the clickedCards stack. Otherwise, the MemoryItem would be lost and won't be available to be reset in case no match is found. This means you also have to track if a match has been found in a class field and use it to decide to restore values back to the stack. That brings us to the conclusion of this chapter; let's take a look at what we've accomplished.

Conclusion

In general, data structures are really outside the scope of introductory programming language texts. However, we're learning by working with full game projects, and it's important to have a basic level of knowledge with regard to them. You really do need data structures to build advanced programs like games, and I want you to be able to build your own games at the conclusion of the text.

What We Covered

In our second foray into the world of data structures, we traversed a fair amount of ground. Let's take a look at a summary of the material.

- Multidimensional Arrays: We took a look at multidimensional arrays even touching about third dimensional arrays and the concept of how fast its memory usage can grow. We saw some examples of how to declare and use the data structure.

- Hashes: Really one of the most powerful tools in programming, hashes allow you to quickly look up data using a key instead of an array index. One use of this data structure is to make dictionary style lookups where a key returns information of some kind.

- Stacks and Queues: A very important set of data structures that maybe aren't used as often as some of the others we've reviewed. Nevertheless, they are a very important tool in any programming language. Similarly, we took a look at basic use cases and functionality.

- Parameterized Types and Data Structures: We took a moment to talk about the configuration we've been doing with the different data structures and their internal data types.

- Challenge: Stacks: We took on one of the most difficult challenges yet, refactoring an entire variable's implementation in the ScreenGame. java file of the `MemoryMatch` class.

Sadly, we won't be reviewing anymore data structures in this text, but we will be taking a look at looping in Chapter 6 and learn different ways we can iterate over the elements of a data structure.

CHAPTER 6

Looping and Iteration

You've built up your coding toolbox, and you have a good selection of powerful tools, including data structures, at your fingertips. One thing that we've looked at in a few code listings but haven't reviewed in detail is how to run code over and over again in a loop.

Looping and iteration, much like flow control, are integral to many Java programs. In fact, we couldn't really have games without them. I'll elaborate on this further when we cover main game loops, in depth, later on in the chapter. For now, let's focus on the fundamentals of looping. The Java programming language gives us three different techniques we can use to employ looping and iteration in our programs. Let's see what we have to work with.

- For Loops: We've seen these a few times in the example listings and coding challenges.

- For-Each Loops: Much like their close counterpart, the for loop, for-each loops follow the same logical structure but are expressed differently.

- Do-While Loops: The outlier in the set of looping constructs, although very useful in certain cases.

I've also mentioned the concept of iteration, and we'll explore this a bit further when we talk about the for-each loop. As it turns out, Java, being a full featured and mature programming language, has the concept of Interfaces. An interface is exactly as it sounds, a set way to interact with something. When applied to data structures, we can define a set way to iterate over them. That is, ask the data structure for the next element in the series if there is one. Next up, we'll take a look at for loops in Java.

© Victor G. Brusca 2023
V. G. Brusca, *Introduction to Java Through Game Development*, https://doi.org/10.1007/978-1-4842-8951-8_6

For Loops

For loops, in my opinion, are the workhorse of looping constructs in Java. They tend to be the go-to solution for most situations that require repeated execution of code in a loop. We'll start the discussion on looping with an introduction to basic for loops.

Basic For Loop

The for loop has two versions. In this section, we'll take a look at the basic version of the for loop, which takes a number of arguments to define the constraints of the loop. Keeping control of loops in your programs is very important. For loops are inherently safer, though you can still abuse them, because they require you to define the starting point and ending point of the loop's iteration. Let's take a look at an example.

Listing 6-1. Example of a Basic For Loop

```
//code
1 for(int i = 0; i < 10; i++) {
2     System.out.print(i + ", ");
3 }

//output
1 Loop Output: 0, 1, 2, 3, 4, 5, 6, 7, 8, 9,
```

An example of a basic for loop with internal index variable, constant length, and simple increment. Notice the elements numbers 0 to 9 and not 1 to 10.

We've encountered the basic for loop a few times in the course of the text, so it should look familiar to you. Let's break down what's actually going on here. The for loop statement has three parts to it and a body. The first part of the for loop is ended by the first semicolon. This space is for initializing loop variables. Variables declared here are only available in the scope of the loop's body, meaning you can't refer to them outside of the loop. For instance, the example shown in Listing 6-2 would cause an error.

Listing 6-2. Example of the Loop Control Variable's Scope

```
1 for(int i = 0; i < 10; i++) {
2     System.out.print(i + ", ");
3 }
4 System.out.println("The last index of the loop was " + i + ".");
```

An example of erroneously accessing the loop control variable outside the scope of the loop.

The second part of the for loop declaration is the definition of the testing condition. This is the condition you set to cause the loop to stop running. Needless to say, this is an important part of the loop's declaration. This part is ended by the second semicolon. The last part of the declaration is the increment/decrement statement. This determines how the loop control variable is adjusted after each loop iteration.

Now that you know all about the different parts of the for loop's declaration, I can tell you that none of them are required. Let's further the discussion with an example.

Listing 6-3. Example of an Empty For Loop

```
1 for(; ;) {
2    System.out.print("Still running...");
3 }
```

An example of an empty for loop. The Java compiler will complain about this loop but only if there is code after it.

What do you think the result of running the for loop from Listing 6-3 will be? If you thought about infinite looping, then you're right. This loop will run infinitely, not a good thing. We like to keep control of our loops when working on games. In general, when programming, you should not have an infinite loop by design. There's no reason why you can't include an escape condition, like so.

Listing 6-4. Example of a For Loop with Escape Condition

```
1 boolean exit = false;
2 for(; exit == true;) {
3    System.out.print("Still running...");
4 }
```

An example of a for loop with only an escape condition defined.

We've covered the basics of for loops at this point, but there are a few subtle details about them that I want to review before we move on to for-each loops. Take a look at the example code in Listing 6-5.

Listing 6-5. A Set of For Loop Examples Using Different Techniques

```
//code
01 System.out.print("Loop #1: ");
02 for (int h = 0; h < 10; h++) {
03     System.out.print(h + ", ");
04 }
05 System.out.println("");
06
07 System.out.print("Loop #2: ");
08 int i;
09 for (i = 0; i < 10; i++) {
10     System.out.print(i + ", ");
11 }
12 System.out.println("");
13
14 System.out.print("Loop #3: ");
15 int j = 0;
16 int len = 10;
17 for (; j < len; j++) {
18     System.out.print(j + ", ");
19 }
20 System.out.println("");
21
22 System.out.print("Loop #4: ");
23 int k = 0;
24 for (; k < len; k++) {
25     System.out.print(k + ", ");
26 }
27 System.out.println("");
28
29 System.out.print("Loop #5: ");
30 int l = 100;
31 int delta = 5;
32 for (; l > 0; l -= delta) {
33     System.out.print(l + ", ");
```

```
34 }
35 System.out.println("");

//output
01 Loop #1: 0, 1, 2, 3, 4, 5, 6, 7, 8, 9,
02 Loop #2: 0, 1, 2, 3, 4, 5, 6, 7, 8, 9,
03 Loop #3: 0, 1, 2, 3, 4, 5, 6, 7, 8, 9,
04 Loop #4: 0, 1, 2, 3, 4, 5, 6, 7, 8, 9,
05 Loop #5: 100, 95, 90, 85, 80, 75, 70, 65, 60, 55, 50, 45, 40, 35, 30,
25, 20, 15, 10, 5,
```

An example of different for loops using different initialization and exit condition variables.

Java Programming Note: Always double-check your loop's exit condition. It is a common source of error and can cause your program to crash or behave unexpectedly.

Take a moment to review the previous listing. There are some important subtle points that adjust how we can utilize for loops. The first example, loop #1 on line 1, is your run-of-the-mill basic for loop. Nothing too interesting going on here. Moving on to loop #2, this loop has a slight adjustment that moves the declaration of the loop control variable outside of the loop. The variable is still initialized in the for loop's declaration, but we can now check to see what value the loop ended on. This actually comes in handy quite often in game programming, so keep it in mind.

Loop #3, line 14, takes this concept a bit further. In this example, we've used a variable in the loop's condition statement instead of using a constant value as in previous examples. That's very interesting. Rarely will you work with loops such that using a constant value in the condition makes sense. Much more often you'll want this to be data driven, and using a variable accomplishes that for us.

Turning your attention to loop #4, the only aspect of this example that is interesting is the fact that the loop control variable is declared and initialized outside of the loop. In this case, we've moved the entire statement out. At this point, moving initialization of the loop control variable may just be a matter of style. It's not functionally different from declaring the variable outside of the loop but initializing it as part of the loop's declaration.

Lastly, we have loop #5. There are actually two things we've never seen before in this for loop. Can you spot them? The first one is that we've declared the loop's delta, the increment/decrement value, outside of the loop. This is in-line with the concept of data driving these values. The second is that this loop counts down, not up. Needless to say, there are a number of permutations of the basic for loop implementation. For the most part though, they are just slight adjustments from the most basic for loop statement. In the next section, we'll take a look at a different kind of for loop: the for-each loop.

For-Each Loop

We spent a fair amount of time reviewing for loops, a new powerful tool in your coding toolbox. In this section, we'll take a look at a cousin of the for loop: the for-each loop. In Java, a common occurrence is to iterate, loop, over the contents of a data structure. This occurs frequently in games to check the state of the game's objects for things like collisions, etc. This is a fairly common occurrence in Java game programming, so let's take a look at an example of iterating over a data structure using a basic for loop and an array, shall we?

Listing 6-6. Example of Iterating over an Array with a For Loop

```
1 int[] ar1 = new int[] { 0,1,2,3,4,5 };
2 int len = ar1.length;
3 for(int i = 0; i < len; i++) {
4     int val = ar1[i];
5     System.out.println("Index: " + val);
6 }
```

An example of using a basic for loop to iterate over an array.

It's not the most interesting example, but there are a few points I'd like to discuss. The first one is that when iterating over the array, we're keeping track of the array index we're looking at by using the loop control variable to pull data out of the array. Notice that we decided to set the value of the len variable to the length of the array and use it in the loop's condition statement.

**Game Programming Note: When iterating over data structures, you often have to get a length or count of items to loop over. In some cases, you might simply add the method call that returns the size of the data structure right in the for loop's declaration. It may be much more efficient to store that value once in a local variable than to calculate it every loop iteration. This depends greatly on the data structure you are using, but it is something you should be aware of.

Now, let's look at the same code, but we'll use a for-each loop instead. A few things should stand out to us. Let's take a look at some code!

Listing 6-7. Example of Iterating over an Array with a For-Each Loop

```
1 int[] ar1 = new int[] { 0,1,2,3,4,5 };
2 for(Integer val : ar1) {
3     System.out.println("Index: " + val);
4 }
```

An example of using a basic for-each loop to iterate over an array. The array can be of any data type; we chose integers to simplify the listing.

I should take a moment to note that the array could contain other data types like String, Object, or other classes. At first look, it seems like a bit of a cleaner implementation of the basic for loop. There are a few important differences. We don't have a loop control variable, nor do we have an exit condition. Because we are iterating over the array directly, using the Enumeration interface, we no longer take direct control of the process. Another small difference is that we're using Integers as opposed to ints, and we've moved the declaration of the variable we use to hold each array element, val, into the loop's declaration itself.

Why do we need a for-each loop if we can do the same thing with a for loop you ask? Well, for-each loops certainly have their place. They are a bit more intuitive when working with data structures, but you have to give up a little bit of control to use them. In any case, they are an important tool for your coding toolbox; keep them in mind when working with data structures. That brings us to the conclusion of the review on for loops. In the next section, we'll take a look at a very important type of loop: the while loop.

While Loops

The next type of loop we'll look at is the while loop. Just like many languages before it, Java supports the while loop, and in our particular case, it is a very important loop indeed. This is because the while loop is the Java looping statement used in a game's main loop. More on that in just a bit. While loops are much lighter than for loops in terms of complexity to declare one. You only have to supply a condition for the loop to exit and a body, if you so choose. Let's take a look at the basic while loop.

Basic While Loop

The basic while loop is leaner declaration than the for loop, but it has some major differences. I've refactored the code from Listing 6-1 to use a while loop.

Listing 6-8. Example of a Basic While Loop

```
//code
1 int i = 0;
2 while(i < 10) {
3    System.out.print(i + ", ");
4    i++;
5 }

//output
1 Loop Output: 0, 1, 2, 3, 4, 5, 6, 7, 8, 9,
```

An example of using a basic while loop to iterate over an array.

You may be asking yourself why do we have while loops if they are just more manual and abstract than for loops. While you can convert between them in probably all cases, for loops lend themselves to indexed iteration over a set of elements. While loops, although they can be configured to accomplish the same task as for loops, are much more suited to running code repeatedly in response to a given state.

Listing 6-9. Example of a Condition-Based While Loop

```
1 while(gameIsRunning) {
2    //place game code here
3 }
```

An example of using a while loop to run code in response to a certain condition.

Another example that really reinforces when a while loop is a better choice than a for loop is when you have to wait for a certain amount of time to pass.

Listing 6-10. Example of a Time Sink While Loop

```
1 long t = System.getCurrentTimeMillis();
2 long end = t + 2000; //2 seconds
3
4 //wait for 2 seconds to pass
5 while(t < end) {
6     t = System.getCurrentTimeMillis();
7 }
```

An example of using a while loop to wait for a certain amount of time to pass.

Notice how strange it would be to express waiting for two seconds using a for loop. The while loop is a much cleaner and intuitive implementation. One last thing before we move on to discuss the most famous while loop of them all: the main game loop. While loops are notorious for causing infinite loops in programs. Always be aware of what causes your while loop's condition to trigger, and double-check your code to avoid any infinite loops.

** Java Programming Note: It's a good idea to place an escape clause into your while loops if you aren't sure they will work properly the first time. To do this, simply create a variable to track loop iterations and a variable set to the maximum number of iterations. Then, not relying the while loop's exit condition, add an if statement to the end of the while loop checking if the current iteration is greater than the maximum. If so, exit out of the loop with a break statement.

That's really all I wanted to say about basic while loops. They are elegant, a bit dangerous, and a powerful tool to add to our coding toolbox. In the next section, we'll talk a little bit about a very important while loop, the main game loop, and its role in video games.

Main Game Loop

The main game loop is just what it sounds like; it's the main loop running the key processes of a video game. Just about every video game has one so I'd be remiss in my duty if we didn't talk about it a bit. There are a few different versions of the main game loop; let me list them here. Let me prefix this topic by saying that the discussion gets a bit advanced. It's more important for me to review this information accurately than to try to simplify it. This is a section you should come back to from time to time.

- Implicit Frame Rate: I know it sounds surprising but why bother adding the extra assembly code to control the frame rate when the hardware is capped at a 25MHz clock frequency? Am I right? In this case, the FPS is set by the limits of the hardware itself.

- Explicit Frame Rate: In this version of the main game loop, you keep track of how much time it took to complete the current frame's work. If there is time left over from the allotted time per frame, then the game waits until this time passes. By waiting, the frame rate is kept near the target FPS instead of increasing to the hardware-supported maximum FPS.

- Frame Rate Independent: With this version of the main game loop, you don't enforce a frame rate at all; it is FPS independent, but you still maintain control over the speed at which the game runs. Instead of an implicit or explicit frame rate, pixels per frame, you look at things in the context of time, pixels per second. To do so, you have to calculate a time delta for the current frame, which I'll show you how to do in just a bit. More on this soon.

We can't really talk about main game loops without talking about frames and frame rates. A frame, in a video game, is one iteration of the game loop. The main responsibilities of the main game loop are as follows:

- Update: Poll hardware for the state of input, update the enemy AI, update the enemy positions, etc. This step in the game loop is where we process the game logic and give it life.

- Draw: Sometimes referred to as "render," the draw step is where all the calculations necessary to represent the game on the screen are performed.

The actual code used to power the game engine's main game loop, used by all the associated game projects, is as follows. We won't review it in depth here, but can you spot where the update and draw work are performed? Here's a hint: look for those words in the code listing and you'll find the associated method calls.

Listing 6-11. MmgGameApiJava Game Engine's Main Game Loop – Game Panel Class

```
01 if (PAUSE == true || EXIT == true) {
02     //do nothing
03 } else {
04     UpdateGame();
05 }
06
07 //update graphics
08 bg = GetBuffer();
09 g = backgroundGraphics;
10
11 if (currentScreen == null || currentScreen.IsPaused() == true ||
   currentScreen.IsReady() == false) {
12     //do nothing
13 } else {
14     //clear background
15     g.setColor(Color.DARK_GRAY);
16     g.fillRect(0, 0, winWidth, winHeight);
17
18     //draw border
19     g.setColor(Color.WHITE);
20     g.drawRect(MmgScreenData.GetGameLeft() - 1, MmgScreenData.
       GetGameTop() - 1, MmgScreenData.GetGameWidth() + 1, MmgScreenData.
       GetGameHeight() + 1);
21
22     g.setColor(Color.BLACK);
23     g.fillRect(MmgScreenData.GetGameLeft(), MmgScreenData.GetGameTop(),
       MmgScreenData.GetGameWidth(), MmgScreenData.GetGameHeight());
24
```

```
25    p.SetGraphics(g);
26    p.SetAdvRenderHints();
27    currentScreen.MmgDraw(p);
28
29    if (MmgHelper.LOGGING == true) {
30        tmpF = g.getFont();
31        g.setFont(debugFont);
32        g.setColor(debugColor);
33        g.drawString(GamePanel.FPS, 15, 15);
34        g.drawString("Var1: " + GamePanel.VAR1, 15, 35);
35        g.drawString("Var2: " + GamePanel.VAR2, 15, 55);
36        g.setFont(tmpF);
37    }
38 }
```

An example of a main game loop's workload. Can you see the place where the frame rate data is updated for display?

Let's start things off with an example of the most basic main game loop, one that has an implied frame rate.

Listing 6-12. Controlling Loop Time and Frame Rate

```
1 while (RunFrameRate.RUNNING == true) {
2     if (RunFrameRate.PAUSE == false) {
3         Update();
4         Redraw();
5     }
6 }
```

An example of a very simple main game loop with frame rate limited by the hardware only.

As you can see in the most basic form of the main game loop, we don't do any work to control the speed of the loop's execution. We simply let it run as fast as it can go. This version of the main game loop isn't as useful as the next two implementations, but it does deserve a spot on our list. There was a time when computer resources were very sparse and using everything you had was barely enough to get the job done and certainly not more so.

Taking the concept of frames and extending the idea, we have the concept of frames per second or how many frames the game or game engine can run in one second. Using seconds is not very efficient when working with times that are always much less than one second, so we'll introduce the use of milliseconds. In almost all cases for smaller, 2D games, ms will suffice as a time measurement metric. Let's take a look at a formula for calculating ms per frame.

Listing 6-13. Calculating Milliseconds per Frame

```
1 long msPerSec = 1000;
2 long targetFrames = 30;
3 long msPerFrame = msPerSec/targetFrames;
```

An example of calculating the ms per frame for a target frame rate, FPS, of 30.

The simple calculation shown in Listing 6-13 is very useful when working with games that expect an explicit frame rate and work with a "pixels per frame" model. In this model, you move objects and perform your updates on the expectation that the game will run a set number of frames a second. Using this approach, you can control how your game performs across different hardware and ensure a consistent user experience.

Let me guess; you're wondering how you control the timing of the game loop. Let me show you how it's done in the included video games. Because they all run on the same Java game engine, they all use the same lower-level library code for their main game loops. It's a subtle point, but the main game loop is sometimes a part of the game engine you're working with and not directly in your control.

Nevertheless, you should be proficient enough in Java programming and game programming in particular to craft all three main game loop types. Let's look at how to soak up some time to control the speed of a game loop.

Listing 6-14. Controlling Loop Time and Frame Rate

```
01 while (RunFrameRate.RUNNING == true) {
02     frameStart = System.currentTimeMillis();
03
04     if (RunFrameRate.PAUSE == false) {
05         mf.Redraw();
06     }
07
```

```
08      frameStop = System.currentTimeMillis();
09      frameTime = (frameStop - frameStart) + 1;
10      aFps = (1000 / frameTime);
11
12      frameTimeDiff = tFrameTime - frameTime;
13      if (frameTimeDiff > 0) {
14          try {
15              Thread.sleep((int) frameTimeDiff);
16          } catch (Exception e) {
17              MmgHelper.wrErr(e);
18          }
19      }
20
21      frameStop = System.currentTimeMillis();
22      frameTime = (frameStop - frameStart) + 1;
23      rFps = (1000 / frameTime);
24      mf.SetFrameRate(aFps, rFps);
25 }
```

An example of using Java's Thread class to sleep for a set time, allowing for the control of the loop's timing.

The are some subtle points in Listing 6-14 I'd like to discuss. First, look at the while loop on line 1; notice the condition of the loop. It's the game's main loop so it's designed to exit when the game ends. Next on line 2, we capture the frame's start time in ms, frameStart. On line 8, we capture the frame's stop time in ms, frameStop. Lines 4–6 are responsible for updating and redrawing the current screen if the game is not paused.

The total time it took to process the frame is calculated on line 9. The core value is incremented by 1 to prevent the inconvenient value of 0. To determine the actual frames per second of the current frame, line 10, we divide 1000ms by the frame time. The timeFrameDiff variable stores the difference between the allotted time for each frame and the actual time. If that value is greater than zero, then we have some extra time on our hands.

To kill some time, we sleep the current thread for the extra time, line 15. The last calculation is to determine the real frame rate, after the time sink. The actual frame rate is based on letting the game run as fast as possible, while the real frame rate measures the rate the game is trying to maintain. Lastly, on line 24, the frame rate values are updated for the current program. You can see these values every time you run an associated game project. From the example main game loop in the previous listing, you can see that this approach tries to control the game's performance by controlling the amount of work done each frame in milliseconds. By controlling the number of frames run each second we control the speed of the game.

This is the "pixels per frame" approach I mentioned earlier. What happens if we let go of the idea of trying to control the frame rate of the game. Well, you'd say that would be a bad idea as the game will run differently on different hardware. Let's come up with a calculation that tells us, given no limit on the loop's execution time, what percentage of a second passed between the current frame time and the last frame time. Let me demonstrate with some code.

Listing 6-15. Calculating the Delta Time Between Frames

```
1 float deltaTime = (frameStart - lastFrameStart) / 1000.0f;
```

An example of calculating the delta time of the current frame. This small factor has to be applied to all update metrics to synchronize them to the same timing.

The delta time or change in time is the difference between the start of this frame and the moment before work started on the last frame. Essentially, we're capturing the time it took to complete an update and dividing it by 1000ms or 1 second. That gives us a small factor that represents a tiny slice of a second. Think about this. We're not controlling frames here. The game can run as fast as it wants. That will result in a very small `deltaTime`. The calculation is simple enough, but looking at it out of context isn't doing wonders for us. Let's take a look at a full implementation.

Listing 6-16. Example of a Frame Rate Independent Main Game Loop

```
1 while (RunFrameRate.RUNNING == true) {
2     frameStart = System.currentTimeMillis();
3
4     float deltaTime = (frameStart - lastFrameStart) / 1000.0f;
5     lastFrameStart = System.currentTimeMillis();
6
7     Update(deltaTime);
8     Draw(deltaTime);
9 }
```

An example implementation of a frame rate independent main game loop. Using this approach requires the consistent use of the deltaTime factor to synchronize timing and movement.

**Game Programming Note: *It's probably not a good idea to declare a variable in your main game loop if you really don't have to. We left this declaration in the listing to enforce the fact that the deltaTime, float, variable is a real number.*

Notice that in the full version of the frame rate independent main game loop, we can see where the timing values are set in relation to the work done on update. In this case, we've included both the update and the draw methods in the timing calculation. That should result in the value of

```
(frameStart - lastFrameStart)
```

being a small number, just a few milliseconds. Dividing a small number by 1000.0ms results in an even smaller number, and this is the delta time value that we now have to apply to all movement, animation, and timing values for the current frame. Basically, anything that changes a certain amount each second now changes only the amount associated with a small portion of a second.

What we've done is change the way the main game loop runs so that we're making small adjustments each game frame in response to the time it took to process the previous frame. This requires making all our update logic time based and not frame based. Let's see what the difference might look like.

Listing 6-17. Example of Frame- and Time-Based Object Movement

```
//frame based
int targetFPS = 60;
int movementPerSecond = 600; //600 pixels
int movementPerFrame = movementPerSecond/targetFPS;
enemy1.moveXY(movementPerFrame);

//time based
movementPerFrame = (int)(movementPerSecond * deltaTime);
enemy2.moveXY(movementPerFrame);
```

An example demonstrating frame-based and time-based movement calculations. Note the use of the deltaTime factor.

That brings us to the conclusion of our discussion on main game loops. I hope you found it interesting and a good application of our while loop knowledge. In the next section, we'll wrap up our review of loops in the Java programming language with the lesser used, but still important, do-while loop.

Do-While Loops

The last loop for us to review in the Java programming language is a bit peculiar. The do-while loop is not used as often as its for and while loop counterparts because it has a certain attribute, which makes it very useful in only a narrow band of circumstances. The do-while loop will always execute at least once. This loop is very similar to the while loop you just reviewed, so we'll cover it quickly.

Basic Do-While Loop

The syntax of the basic do-while loop is demonstrated in Listing 6-18.

Listing 6-18. Example of a Do-While Main Game Loop

```
//basic do-while loop
do {
    //work to do each frame
} while (RunFrameRate.RUNNING == true);
```

An example of a do-while loop–based main game loop. This will get you kicked out of some places.

Although I would actually never use one, I do intend for my game to run at least once, so maybe it's not so crazy to use a do-while loop as your main game loop. Nope, it's crazy; stick to the while loop. There's really nothing more to it. Just keep in mind that this loop will execute once before the condition is checked. Otherwise, you can think of it exactly like you would a while loop.

Break and Continue

We can't talk about looping without talking about the break and continue statements. These are loop control statements that allow you to explicitly exit a loop or jump to the next iteration of the loop if the condition allows for one. It's much easier to demonstrate this than to describe it, so let's motivate this discussion with a code sample.

Listing 6-19. Example of Using Break and Continue for Loop Control

```
01 //basic while loop with loop control
02 while (RunFrameRate.RUNNING == true) {
03     if (PAUSE == true) {
04         continue;
05     } else {
06         UpdateGame();
07         DrawGame();
08     }
09
10     if(EXIT == true) {
11         break;
12     }
13 }
```

An example of a while loop with loop control using the break and continue statement.

As you can see from the example, we can use the break and continue statements to control how the while loop behaves. In this case, we're skipping to the next iteration of the loop if the PAUSE Boolean is set to true. The continue statement does this for us. Similarly, the break statement is used to exit the loop in the case that the EXIT Boolean is set to true.

We could have accomplished the same behavior with some variables and a slightly different structure of the loop's body. The benefit here is how quick and intuitive it is to control your loop using these statements. Keep these in mind when you need to skip a loop iteration or to escape one. Don't abuse them; just like anything else, use them in moderation.

Challenge: For-Each Loops

In this chapter's only coding challenge, you'll have to rely on your newly gained knowledge and coding tools to accomplish the request. Take a look at the following description and clue. Refer back to the text if you have any questions working with for-each loops. Good luck!

Packages Involved:

```
net.middlemind.PongClone_Chapter6_Challenge1
net.middlemind.PongClone_Chapter6_Challenge1_Solved
```

Description:

One of the senior programmers noticed the use of a basic for loop in the MmgDraw method. Refactor the code in this method to use a for-each loop. If done correctly, the game should function normally without error. You must run this package's file – MemoryMatch.java; right-click and select Run File to test the game.

Clue:

Recall from our review of for loops that a for-each loop is similar to a for loop except that it declares its own temporary variable and is only used to loop over the contents of a data structure. Try and write the declaration for the new for-each loop right above or below the existing loop so that you can compare the two as you code. As an added hint, there is a specific listing in the text that demonstrates converting a for loop to a for-each loop. Search for "CHAPTER 6 CHALLENGE 1 SOLUTION" to find all the solution text in the solved project's file.

Challenge Solution

The solution to this challenge takes place in the MmgDraw method, and it requires a standard for to for-each loop conversion plus a little extra care to make sure the Boolean flag is set properly. That's all there is to it. Take your time when working on these challenges, and as always, run the local version of the game's static main, MemoryMatch. java, to test your work. If you converted the loop but your cards aren't flipping back over, check that you're setting the flipped field properly in the MmgDraw method.

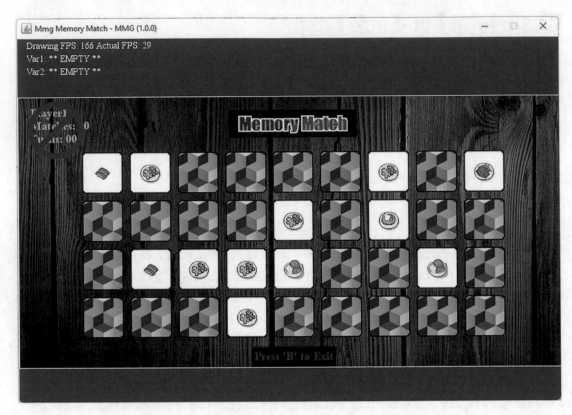

Image 6-1. *Memory Match with a Refactored For Loop in the MmgDraw Method*

A screenshot of the copy of the game used in this challenge. After refactoring the code, the game runs as expected.

That brings us to the conclusion of this section. Take a moment to play the game once you've successfully completed the coding challenge. Make sure the game functions as expected.

Conclusion

That brings us to the end of the chapter on looping and iteration. There's actually a fair amount of more material to cover on the subject of looping. For instance, why were we able to plug in just about any data structure into a for-each loop declaration? I might have made some small mention of this, but we couldn't cover it in detail here. You'll get an understanding of what's happening behind the scenes when you review object-oriented programming in Java over the next two chapters. For now, let's look at a synopsis of the material reviewed in this chapter.

What We Covered

During our exploration of looping and iteration in the Java programming language, we managed to look at all three standard looping mechanisms in Java – the for, while, and do-while loops. We took care to review the most famous loop of all: the main game loop. And we even got to look at the three most common implementations of main game loops. Let me briefly summarize the topics.

- Basic For Loops: We looked at how to declare basic for loops and how the subtle use of variables declared outside of the loop can change how we interact with counting and loop control variables.

- Basic For-Each Loops: We juxtaposed for loops with for-each loops refactoring some earlier code to use the new looping construct. We got to see how clean and intuitive for-each loops can be.

- Basic While Loops: We worked with basic while loops looking at the difference between them and for loops and indicating the different use cases that require a while loop as opposed to a for loop.

- Main Game Loops: In this chapter, we reviewed three of the most common types of main game loops: implicit frame rate, explicit frame rate, and frame rate independent.

- Do-While Loops: Although many might consider it an antiquated feature of the language, if you happen to be working in a solution space where loops iterate at least once, it can be a life saver. Our brief review coupled with the sections on while loops should give you a solid foundation to build on.

- Break and Continue Statements: No review on Java looping would be complete without a discussion about the break and continue statements. We quickly reviewed this topic and exemplified their use.

Now that we've covered looping and added a whole new set of tools to our coding toolbox, we're ready to take on one of the more advanced aspects of the Java programming language: object-oriented programming. You have a good amount of experience and a solid foundation to build on; consider object-oriented programming just one more tool to add to your toolbox. Enjoy!

CHAPTER 7

Objects, Classes, and OOP

You've increased your experience working with the Java programming language over the last few chapters, and now we've reached the more advanced topic of OOP, object-oriented programming. Java is, first and foremost, an object-oriented programming language. Whether you were aware of it or not, you have been using classes and OO, object-oriented, programming throughout almost the entire text, essentially starting with data structures.

That fact right there should put you at ease if you find the subject matter too intimidating. Let's take a shot at a simple definition of OOP in Java. First, you define your class in a Java class file of the same name. For instance, if you created a new class to manage a spaceship, the file might be named

```
SpaceShip.java
```

And you would use this class in the most basic way, like so:

```
SpaceShip testShip = new SpaceShip();
```

That's really all there is to it. At the most basic level, classes are a way for you to model something. How do we model something on a computer? We collect and track data. Sometimes, that data is an image that actually looks like a spaceship; sometimes, it's just numbers that describe the attributes of a spaceship; and sometimes, it's both.

The main takeaway here is that the classes you define when used in a program become instances of classes or objects. Not to be confused with the super-class of all Java classes: the Object class. Now, think about all the different data structures we've reviewed together. Recall the angled brackets that are used to define the internal data type of the data structure. Using the SpaceShip class to further the discussion, let's look at using it with a data structure:

© Victor G. Brusca 2023
V. G. Brusca, *Introduction to Java Through Game Development*, https://doi.org/10.1007/978-1-4842-8951-8_7

```
//the ArrayList class from the java.util package
ArrayList<SpaceShip> enemyShips = new ArrayList<>();
```

That's interesting. By using our custom classes with classes that come with Java, we can create new combinations that help us model all sorts of different problems. For instance, in the previously shown code snippet, we could be trying to find a way to track the current level's enemy ships in a new 2D space shooter we're working on. Now that you have the basic understanding of what a class is and how it might be used in a Java program, let's take a look at how to properly define a class in Java.

Classes

To start our discussion on Java classes, let's take a look at the definition of a class from Java's documentation[1]:

"A class is a blueprint or prototype from which objects are created."

The definition brings up some interesting concepts. For one thing, it alludes to the idea that the classes you define are used to create something, objects. We've talked about objects a bit before, but let's start thinking of them as an instance of a class and let's keep in mind that a class has a file somewhere, with the same name as the class and with a .java file extension. That is the general nature of classes in the Java programming language. Let's understand a bit more about them and how to start defining our own. In general, the definition for a class in Java can contain the following pieces of information:

- Access Modifiers: A class can be public or private, or use the default access modifier.

- Class Keyword: The `class` keyword is used to create a class.

- Class Name: The name should begin with a letter, and in Java, the letter is usually capitalized.

- Superclass (optional): The name of the class' parent (superclass), if any, preceded by the keyword extends. A class can only extend (subclass) one parent.

---

[1]https://docs.oracle.com/javase/tutorial/java/concepts/index.html

- Interfaces (optional): A comma-separated list of interfaces implemented by the class, if any, preceded by the keyword implements. A class can implement more than one interface. Think of the Enumerable interface we mentioned earlier.

- Body: The class body is surrounded by braces, {}. This is where the class' members – including fields, methods, and constructors – are defined.

Let's focus on how to declare a class. As such, we'll look at class extension and interfaces in the next chapter. For now, we'll focus on access modifiers and the basic class declaration. Let me show you a few versions of a standard class declaration, and we'll review their differences afterward.

Listing 7-1. Example of Simple Class Declarations

```
01 package org.learn_java.classes;
02
03 //class #1, public access
04 public class SimpleClassPublic { ... }
05
06 //class #2, default access
07 class SimpleClassDefault { ... }
08
09 //class #3, error not allowed for top-level classes
10 protected class SimpleClassProtected { ... }
11
12 //class #4, error not allowed for top-level classes
13 private class SimpleClassPrivate { ... }
```

A listing showing a few correct, simple class declarations followed by two incorrect declarations. You cannot use the protected or private modifier on a top-level class.

In Listing 7-1, there are a number of example, simple class declarations. The first two are valid declarations because they specify default or public class access. The last two are invalid; you'll get a compiler error and use access modifiers protected and private. Java doesn't like it if you use those access modifiers on a top-level class declaration. Let me summarize the modifiers you can use for a top-level class declaration here:

- public: The class is accessible by any other class.

- default: The class is only accessible by classes in the same package. This is used when you don't specify a modifier. Packages are provided as a way for you to organize your classes. In general, classes that are related belong in the same package.

The default access modifier is also called package-private, which means that all members are visible within the same package but aren't accessible from other packages. Now that we know how to declare a class, in the most basic form, let's take a look at how we can customize the class. In general, classes are a means to create a model of something. As such, you need to be able to associate certain data with an instance of your class. Class fields give you a way to do just that. Let's take a look!

Fields

In Java, fields are variables of a certain data type that are associated with a class. An attribute is another name sometimes given to them, but it's usually reserved for public class fields specifically. A brief demonstration will go a long way to furthering your understanding of class fields. Let's bring back a listing from Chapter 4, an example of a basic Java class.

Listing 7-2. Example of a Basic Java Class – Originally Listing 4-18

```
01 public class GameData {
02     public State gameState = State.NONE;
03     public int numberOfPlayers = 1;
04     public boolean gameOver = false;
05     public String playerName = "AAA";
06 }
07
08 public GameData gameMetaData;
09 gameMetaData = new GameData();
```

An example of a custom data type defined through a Java class. Notice the use of fields to hold data associated with the class.

In Listing 7-2, the GameData class has four fields of varying data types. All the fields have the public access modifier, so they can be accessed by any other class. In Java, all code is contained in a class at some level, so all access control is class based. Let's demonstrate using the class' fields before we discuss the other access modifiers available to us when defining a class. In the next listing, I'll adjust the modifiers used with the class and its fields. See if you can figure out the access levels defined by the declaration.

Listing 7-3. Example of a Basic Java Class with Various Access Modifiers

```
01 class GameData {
02     State gameState = State.NONE;
03     public int numberOfPlayers = 1;
04     protected boolean gameOver = false;
05     private String playerName = "AAA";
06 }
07
08 public GameData gameMetaData = new GameData();
```

An example of a Java class that uses various access modifiers for both the class itself and the class' fields.

Listing 7-3 uses the default access modifier for the GameData class. This is a slight adjustment from Listing 7-2, which used the public access modifier. Similarly, the class fields have been updated to use the default, public, protected, and private access modifiers, respectively. Sure, we could have set them all to public and left the responsibility up to the programmer to make sure the class fields were used properly.

This is another example of leaving a responsibility to the developer that could be managed by the Java compiler. For instance, why worry about correct and consistent use of the class' variables when we can enforce the desired use in the class definition itself. Let's say that the player's name is sacred. In our game, once the player's name is set, we don't want it changing.

To enforce this, we use the private access modifier on the playerName variable on line 5. Now the variable can't be changed by just any code. Because it's private, it can now only be changed by the GameData class itself using a class method, constructor, or variable default, as shown in Listing 7-3. The protected access modifier, line 4, is used to allow access to fields that meet the following criteria:

- Any code within the enclosing class

- Other classes in the same package as the enclosing class

- Subclasses, classes that extend this class, regardless of packages

Remember, packages are Java's way of organizing classes. Declaring what package your class belongs to is as simple as adding the following line to the top of your class' java file:

```
package org.learn_java.classes;
```

This means that the Java class' source file can be found in the following directory structure local to the Java project's source directory. The package and the location of the file are connected. Keep this in mind when you're trying to track down classes in your project.

```
./src
-> org
    -> learn_java
        -> classes
            -> GameData.java
```

Java Programming Note: Not all Java IDEs will use the same project structure. Take the time to get to know the structure of the projects that your Java IDE creates and have a clear understanding of where your packages and Java class files reside.

Think about how you might use this access modifier in your own programs. What situations can you imagine where you want to limit access to package classes, etc.? There's no right or wrong answer here, just food for thought. Moving on to the next variable on line 3, `numberOfPlayers`. This variable has a `public` access modifier and can be accessed from any other class.

Listing 7-4. Example of Accessing a Public Field of a Basic Java Class

```
//code
1 public GameData gameMetaData = new GameData();
2 System.out.println("Number of Players: " + gameMetaData.numberOfPlayers);

//output
1 Number of Players: 1
```

When accessing public fields, you only need to specify the properly instantiated class instance, gameMetaData in this case, and use the dot operator, ".", to specify the public field you want to access.

__Game Programming Note: Using simple classes with public fields is perfectly normal in a Java game implementation. Start worrying about controlling field access more when you need to know that a field's value is changing. Then you can define methods to interact with the field and refactor your existing code if need be.

As you can see, the public access modifier is very simple and offers unrestricted access to a class' variable. In most cases, and if you're not sure what access you really need, you can start off using the public access modifier. Look how easy it is to reference a value using a field of this type, line 2 in the code section of the previous listing. The last access modifier we have to discuss is the case where none is provided, the default access modifier. The default modifier allows access under the following conditions:

- Any code within the enclosing class

- Other classes in the same package as the enclosing class

This is not too different than the protected access modifier except that it doesn't allow access to subclasses, or classes that extend the current class unless they are in the same package. That brings us to the conclusion of the section on class fields. They are a powerful tool to add to your coding toolbox as you will now be able to create classes that not only support tracking certain data but can also control access to that data by using Java's access modifiers. In the next section, we'll take a look at another very important part of a class, its methods.

Methods

Methods are another type of class member, meaning they are always defined within the context of a class definition. Methods in Java are similar to functions in other programming languages, like C and C++. They are blocks of code that only run when called. They can receive parameters and can return a value.

Up until now, I've avoided discussing the concept of scope as it's a more advanced programming concept that has less to do with the nuances of the language itself than more to do with the structure of the language elements in any given case. Variables in

Java have a scope. The scope of a variable is the block, or blocks of code, where that variable is valid and accessible.

Fields in Java have a scope just like other variables do, and you can access them not only from outside the class, as we saw in Listing 7-4, but also inside the class in methods. This allows you to create reusable blocks of code that work with the class' fields, and any parameters passed to the method, to generate a return value, if need be. Methods can in fact take no parameters and return no data. Let's further this discussion with a few examples of different method declarations. We'll keep working with the fictional GameData class we've used in the previous two listings. Let's jump into some code!

Listing 7-5. Example of Different Class Method Declarations

```
01 class GameData {
02     public enum State {
03         NONE,
04         GAME_ON,
05         GAME_OFF
06     }
07
08     State gameState = State.NONE;
09     public int numberOfPlayers = 1;
10     protected boolean gameOver = false;
11     private String playerName = "AAA";
12
13     State getGameState() {
14         return this.gameState;
15     }
16
17     void setGameState(State newState) {
18         this.gameState = newState;
19     }
20
21     public int getNumberOfPlayers() {
22         return numberOfPlayers;
23     }
24
```

```
25      public void setNumberOfPlayers(int p) {
26          numberOfPlayers = p;
27      }
28
29      protected boolean getGameOver() {
30          return gameOver;
31      }
32
33      protected Boolean getGameOver2() {
34          return gameOver;
35      }
36
37      public void setGameOver(boolean b) {
38          gameOver = b;
39      }
40
41      public void setGameOver2(Boolean b) {
42          gameOver = b;
43      }
44
45      public String getPlayerName() {
46          return this.internalGetPlayerName();
47      }
48
49      public void setPlayerName(String pName) {
50          this.internalSetPlayerName(pName);
51      }
52
53      private String internalGetPlayerName() {
54          return this.playerName;
55      }
56
57      private void internalSetPlayerName(String pName) {
58          this.playerName = pName;
59      }
60 }
```

A complete listing of the fictional GameData class showing the State enumeration, fields, and class get/set methods.

Take a close look at the listing and make sure to identify which access modifier is used where; we'll go over the class and each method in detail now. As you can see from the class declaration, the default access modifier is used. This means that the class is package-private. On line 2, the State enumeration is public. Recall from our review of data types that an enumeration is a type of custom data type that is specialized for a list of unique values.

In this case, we have a very simple implementation with only three values: NONE, GAME_ON and GAME_OFF. The class variables are declared on lines 8–11; note that they are assigned explicit default values. If none were explicitly expressed, Java will provide a language default. The first method for us to look at starts on line 13. It uses the default access modifier and takes no arguments. The naming convention used by the method indicates that it's a "get" method.

It is a common convention in Java to write get/set methods to open up access to protected class fields. This gives you the benefit of centralization, and you can track, trace, and debug access to the field easily via its get and set methods. This method returns the value of the class' gameState variable. In the next method, we provide a means for setting the value of the gameState variable, line 17. This class method also uses the default access modifier and returns no value.

To indicate that a method does not return a value, we use the void keyword in place of a return data type. There's a subtle new Java feature hidden in these two methods. Can you spot it? Direct your attention to the gameState variable and how it is referenced in each method body. The keyword, this, is used to reference the current instance of the class. The actual class instance doesn't exist yet, but when this class is used in a Java program, the this keyword will resolve to the current instance of the class.

It's common to use the this keyword in class methods as it intuitively indicates which variables are in fact class fields. The next pair of methods for us to look at is the get and set methods for the numberOfPlayers variable, on lines 21–27. In this case, the methods have a slight variation in their declaration as they are both explicitly set to public and do not use the this keyword when referencing variables.

If you haven't guessed by now, class methods can have the same access modifiers as class fields. The getNumberOfPlayers and setNumberOfPlayers methods are publically available; then any class can access them. The next two methods we'll look at are slightly different versions of the same method, but their difference is important. Can you spot the subtle nuance I'm referring to? If you were about to say the use of the Boolean data type instead of boolean, then you're correct.

This is an example of the automatic "boxing" and "unboxing" that Java does for you with regard to the basic data types and their boxed counterparts. And here you thought this section would only have information about class methods. Many things in the Java programming language are tied together or have interesting little overlaps. Both the getGameOver and getGameOver2 methods have the protected access modifier and specify boolean return types.

Take a moment to look over the setGameOver and setGameOver2 methods. Notice the same nuance with regard to the use of Boolean and boolean data types in the method parameters. The last two methods are another special case for us to review. The playerName variable, line 11, is private, and as such, it cannot be accessed outside of the current class. In this case, we've created a public pair of get and set methods that handle providing access to the private class field.

Note that these methods use a pair of private, internal, class methods – internalGetPlayerName and internalSetPlayerName – to do the actual work of updating the class field. This is an example of using private methods to control access to certain class functionality, which consequently falls under encapsulation. That brings us to the end of the method review of Listing 7-5, but there's still a fair amount I'd like to discuss on this topic. Let's take a look at a few more methods of the GameData class. These examples will demonstrate some new concepts with regard to defining class methods.

Listing 7-6. More Examples of Different Method Declarations – GameData Class

```
//code
01 public void setAll(State state, int playerCount, boolean gameOverFlag,
   String name) {
02     gameState = state;
03     numberOfPlayers = playerCount;
04     gameOver = gameOverFlag;
05     playerName = name;
06 }
07
08 public void testVariableScope() {
09     int numberOfPlayers = 2;
10     System.out.println("Local variable number of players: " +
       numberOfPlayers);
```

```
11      System.out.println("Class field number of players: " + this.
        numberOfPlayers);
12 }
13
14 //example of using the vararg method parameter feature
15 public void setAll(Object ... objs) {
16     if(objs.length >= 4) {
17         gameState = (State)objs[0];
18         numberOfPlayers = (Integer)objs[1];
19         gameOver = (Boolean)objs[2];
20         playerName = (String)objs[3];
21     } else {
22         System.err.println("Incorrect number of parameters found!");
23     }
24 }

//output
01 Local variable number of players: 2
02 Class field number of players: 1
```

A number of new method declarations demonstrating an aspect of class methods such as multiple method parameters, method variable scope, and the Java language's vararg feature.

In Listing 7-6, I've shown some of the subtle details of declaring class methods. On line 1, the setAll method takes a number of parameters of different data types and uses them to initialize the class' fields. Next, on line 8, the testVariableScope method is used to demonstrate declaring a local method variable that hides a class field. In this case, the numberOfPlayers variable is declared both locally and as a class field.

In situations like this where the variable is referenced without the "this" keyword, the local variable is used; otherwise, the class field is used. This method and its output demonstrate how a local method variable can hide a class field. Make sure the output makes sense to you before moving on. The last method in this group, line 15, is an example of a little used feature of the Java programming language feature: the vararg modifier.

Adding an ellipsis, . . ., after a method parameter tells the Java compiler that the parameter will be passed in as an array of the given data type, in this case, an array of Objects. Notice how we check the length of the array parameter, and if enough values exist, we cast them out of the array and set the class fields. While this is a powerful feature of the Java programming language that has its place with certain methods, this is a tool you shouldn't find yourself using too often.

If you are using it frequently, you should ask yourself what it is you're trying to do and think about another implementation strategy. At this point in our review, you should be comfortable with declaring classes and defining different class fields and methods. But all of these class members require a valid instance of a class to use them. How can we create an attribute of the class that is shared by all instances of the class?

This is where the static keyword comes in handy.

Static Members

The Java programming language supports defining class members that exist, uniquely, for each instance of the class. We've seen these before; they are class fields. Java also supports defining class members that exist for the class itself and for each instance of the class. Let me quickly review the concepts of declaration and instantiation with regard to classes so that we can see the importance of static class members.

Listing 7-7. Declaring and Instantiating Class Instances

```
01 GameData gameData1;//declaration
02 gameData1 = new GameData();//initialization
03 gameData1.setAll(State.NONE, 0, true, "");
04
05 GameData gameData2 = new GameData();//instantiation
06 gameData2.setAll(State.NONE, 0, true, "");
07
08 GameData gameData3;//uninitialized
09 gameData3.setAll(State.NONE, 0, true, "");//error this class instance
   isn't initialized
10
11 //setting a static class field
12 GameData.MAX_NUM_PLAYERS = 2;
```

```
13
14 //calling a static class method
15 GameData.SetMaxNumPlayers(2);
```

An example demonstrating declaring, initializing, and instantiating classes. Note that we can use static class members without any declaration, initialization, or instantiation.

In Listing 7-7, we have three examples of working with class methods followed by two examples that demonstrate using static class members. On lines 1–3, we can see the declaration and initialization of the gameData1 variable. Once the class instance, object, is ready, we can then call its setAll method with some parameters. In a similar fashion, on lines 5–6, we have a slightly more condensed version of the same process. The variable gameData2 is instantiated, declared, and initialized in one line, on line 5, leaving the variable ready to use. A call to the setAll method is made on line 6. In both cases, we could only use the method once an instance of the class had been properly declared and initialized. Lines 8–9 are a demonstration of what not to do. This code will throw an error; you can't call the method of an uninitialized object.

Now we get to the really interesting part. On line 12, we have an example of a static class field. They are very similar to the class fields you have reviewed thus far except that they are prefixed with the static keyword. The static keyword makes the new field a member of the class itself and not of a class instance. What does this mean? Well, it means that you can access the field without any prior code.

As you can see on line 12, we're setting the value of a static class field, but we aren't using a variable; we haven't declared or initialized anything. In this case, we're using the name of the class itself. A static class field belongs to the class and can be accessed from the name of the class itself. Just like with class fields, there is a static version of class methods. Together they constitute the pair of static class members supported by the Java programming language.

On line 15 of Listing 7-7, you can see the use of a static class method. In general, static fields and methods should be capitalized to show that they are different from normal fields and methods, but this is just a convention. I recommend sticking to it though; it will make your code that much more intuitive. We've seen how we can use static class members and how they are different from the normal class members we've worked with thus far, but we haven't seen exactly how we declare them. Let's take a look at how to define static class members by adding some to our fictional GameData class.

Listing 7-8. Example of Static Class Members – GameData Class

```
1 class GameData {
2     public static int MAX_NUM_PLAYERS = 5;
3     public static void SetMaxNumPlayers(int i) {
4         GameData.MAX_NUM_PLAYERS = i;
5     }
6
7     ...
8 }
```

A static class field and a static class method added to the GameData class. The remainder of the fictional GameData class has been abridged in this listing.

**Java Programming Note: It's good practice to not only use capitalized variable names for a class' static fields, you should also place them at the very start of your class' definition. With regard to static methods, there isn't as strong a precedence, although using capitalized method names is common. There isn't an equivalent practice with regard to the placement of static methods, but I like to keep them grouped together and near the start of the class' body.

Static class members, fields and methods, are very similar to normal class fields and methods, and as such, you can use all the same access modifiers. The only caveat there is pertains to the use of static class methods. You cannot directly access other class fields or methods unless they are also `static`, or you have an instance of the class at hand. What does this mean? Well, it means that if you're accessing a static method, that static method can only access other static methods and fields because it is associated with the class itself, not a class instance. Let me further this discussion with a brief example.

Listing 7-9. Example of Static Class Method Usage

```
1 public static void SetMaxNumPlayers(int i) {
2     this.numberOfPlayers = i; //incorrect
3     GameData.MAX_NUM_PLAYERS = i; //correct
4 }
```

This listing has an error. You cannot access a class field, numberOfPlayers, because no class instance is present when accessing a static class member.

Can you spot the issue with the code in Listing 7-9? If you thought that accessing the class field from a static method might be an issue, you thought right. That brings us to the conclusion of the section on static class members. They are an important tool in your coding toolbox and especially come in handy when setting up information associated with the class itself and not an instance.

Constructors

Up to this point in the text, we've used very basic class initialization. For the most part, we've seen declaration and initialization, or instantiation followed by directly setting the class fields or using class methods to do so. While this is certainly a direct and intuitive way to configure our class instances, it can get a bit cumbersome. Imagine working with a class that has 10 or 20 fields that need to be properly initialized?

We could do it with the tools we have in a few different ways. One way would be to explicitly set each class field to the desired value. Another way would be to call some sort of initialization method, not unlike the setAll method we experimented with when working with the fictional GameData class. Let's explore that idea a bit more. Requiring a developer to call a specific method to properly initialize a class doesn't sound too terrible.

Again, we're at a point where we've pushed the responsibility onto the developer, who probably has enough to worry about. Instead, let's push that responsibility onto Java and not worry about it. Let's take a look at a feature of the Java programming language we've been using without really knowing: the class constructor. I'll provide an example to motivate the discussion.

Listing 7-10. Example of Using Class Constructors for Initialization

```
1 GameData gameData1 = new GameData();
2 gameData1.setAll(State.NONE, 0, true, "");
3
4 GameData gameData2 = new GameData(State.NONE, 0, true, "");
```

A listing demonstrating the use of a custom constructor to initialize a class upon instantiation as opposed to the setAll class method.

There is a subtle but powerful distinction between the two ways we've initiated the fictional GameData class in the previous listing. In one case, lines 1–2, we're requiring the developer to know they have to use the setAll method and when. In the second example, line 4, we're using a custom constructor to set the required data for this instance of the GameData class, gameData2. The benefit of this approach is that it's more intuitive and requires less special knowledge on how to configure the class. As the developer, you've provided a constructor that will configure the class for the developer. Let's take a look at how to define custom constructors for our classes.

Listing 7-11. Example of Using Default vs. Custom Class Constructors

```
//class definitions
01 class SimpleClass1 {
02     public int simpleField1;
03 }
04
05 class SimpleClass2 {
06     public int simpleField1;
07     public boolean simpleField2;
08
09     public SimpleClass2() {
10         simpleField1 = 0;
11         simpleField2 = false;
12     }
13
14     public SimpleClass2(int i, boolean b) {
15         simpleField1 = i;
16         simpleField2 = b;
17     }
18 }

//class usage
01 //default constructor is always available
02 SimpleClass1 simp1 = new SimpleClass1();
03
04 //explicitly declared simple constructor
05 SimpleClass2 simp2 = new SimpleClass2();
```

```
06
07 //re-initialization using the custom constructor
08 simp2 = new SimpleClass2(1, true);
```

A demonstration of using default constructors and custom constructors in a class definition.

In Listing 7-11, we're introduced to two simple classes. The first class has only a field and no constructor defined. When we create an instance of this class, line 2, we are using the default constructor. Java takes care of providing a default constructor when you don't explicitly declare one. What happens if we do define a custom constructor? Take a look at the second class definition, SimpleClass2, on line 5. Note that this class defines two constructors.

The first constructor is a re-creation of the default constructor. We have to do this if we decide to define a custom constructor because Java will no longer provide the default constructor once a custom constructor is defined. The use of a default constructor could lead to an incorrectly configured class and errors, so in order to support it, in this case, you have to explicitly create it yourself. You can see our implementation on lines 9–12 and the custom constructor on lines 14–17.

We can now use SimpleClass2's custom constructor, which lets us provide values for the class' fields, or we can use an empty constructor that will mimic the default constructor, line 5 of the class usage section. Keep in mind that you can create as many custom constructors as you need for your class, but don't overuse this capability. You'll end up with very confusing classes to instantiate. That brings us to the end of this section. Time for a coding challenge to reinforce the material we've covered so far.

Challenge: The MmgBmp Class

In this coding challenge, we'll use our newly acquired Java class skills and get to know a little bit more about the game engine and drawing images in the book's included games. Because they are all built on the same game engine, any knowledge you learn with regard to it can be applied equally to all included games.

One of the core aspects of a 2D game engine is the ability to draw images on the screen. Our game engine uses the MmgBmp class to handle this task. In this challenge, we'll get to know this class a bit more and see it in action. Keep in mind all the aspects of class definitions and object-oriented programming that we've covered here as you work through the challenge. Enjoy!

Packages Involved:

```
net.middlemind.MemoryMatch_Chapter7_Challenge1
net.middlemind.MemoryMatch_Chapter7_Challenge1_Solved
```

Description:

Find the package, net.middlemind.MemoryMatch_Chapter7_Challenge1, and open the ScreenGame.java file. In this challenge, you won't be solving any problems for someone else; you'll be having a little fun adding a graphic to the video game that displays at a certain position on the screen and only on certain game states. You can provide your own image, or you can use one of the included images. The images for this game project are stored in the following folder:

```
.\ MemoryMatch\cfg\drawable\MemoryMatch
```

You can use a png or jpg image of your own. The image should be around 200×200 pixels if you're providing one. Simply copy and paste the image into the directory mentioned previously and make sure to remember the name of the image file. If you don't have one of your own, just pick an image out of the directory and keep its name in mind.

Locate the LoadResources folder and find an example of the code used to load your own image into an MmgBmp class field in one of the initialization methods. Add your own image variable named myImg to the class and initialize it near the bottom of the LoadResources method. You'll also need to set the image's position using the SetPosition method and add the image to a container, MmgContainer, in the class so that it can be properly configured for display. You'll get to know the MmgBmp class and some of its fields and methods as you complete this challenge.

In order to display the new image, you must add code to the SetState method for the SHOW_GAME game state. Take a look at the code in the method and specifically how images are shown and hidden depending on the current game state. Add your new image into the mix and follow the precedent set by the current code. Lastly, you'll need to clean things up. Find the UnloadResources method and make sure to clean up your resources by setting the myImg class field to null. You must run this package's file – MemoryMatch.java; right-click and select Run File to test the game.

Clue:

If you run into trouble, stop and take a moment to clear your mind. Look for an existing class field of the MmgBmp data type and trace how it's used in the methods listed in this coding challenge. You can follow the same example except using your chosen file name when loading the image.

Challenge Solution

This solution required you to add code to five places in the `ScreenGame.java` class and potentially to add a new image to the project. It is by far the most complex solution yet, and it requires you to understand class fields and methods involved. What is more, it gives you more experience working with the `MmgBmp` class. The locations where you have to add new code are as follows:

1. Class header: A new class field, `myImg`, of the `MmgBmp` data type has to be added to the class at the bottom of the current list of class fields.

2. LoadResources: A new block of code has to be added near the bottom of the `LoadResources` method. This code should be based on existing image loading code that's in the method but should be adjusted to load your chosen image and store it in the `myImg` field.

3. Positioning and Container: You must set a position for the image using the `SetPosition` method, and the image must be added to one of the `MmgContainer` fields in the class. You can experiment with different containers to see how it affects the visibility of the image.

4. SetState: In this method, you have to make two adjustments. One at the beginning of the method when cleaning up the `SHOW_GAME` state. The second change is lower down in the method, and it requires you to make your image visible when changing to the `SHOW_GAME` state.

5. UnloadResources: The last change you have to make is to clean up after yourself by setting the `myImg` field to null in this method.

While the list of changes seems daunting, it's actually very attainable, and there is a lot of example code you can use as a basis for your code changes. The end result of this coding challenge should be a visible image, of your choice, displayed on the in-game screen. There is a fair amount of room for interpretation here, so have some fun with it!

Challenge: The ScreenGame Class

In order to make your own games using the game engine, you'll need to understand how to load image resources; we've got that covered; you'll also need to understand how to animate the image and how to respond to user input; to that end, we'll be working with the ScreenGame class in this coding challenge.

In this challenge, we'll build off of the work we did in the previous challenge. This is the second time the code base for our challenge will be the solution to the previous challenge. Make sure you've completed the previous challenge successfully and double-check the solution if need be. You've added a new image to the game screen, and now we're going to wire up some controls for it. Let's take a look at the challenge!

Packages Involved:

```
net.middlemind.MemoryMatch_Chapter7_Challenge2
net.middlemind.MemoryMatch_Chapter7_Challenge2_Solved
```

Description:

Find the package, net.middlemind.MemoryMatch_Chapter7_Challenge2, and open the ScreenGame.java file. We'll continue on the same track and implement our own code to experiment with animating, moving an image in response to user input. Choose four different keyboard keys that aren't used by the game. Two of these keys will be used to toggle your new image's visibility. The other two will be used to move your image left and right.

In order to handle user input, you'll need to check for your target keys in the following methods:

- ProcessKeyPress

- ProcessKeyRelease

It's up to you to use the GetPosition, SetPosition methods of the MmgBmp class to control the image's position. You'll also need to use the GetIsVisible, SetIsVisible methods to control the image's visibility. You should be familiar with the keyboard methods and the MmgBmp class methods from your experience using the class in previous challenges.

Clue:

You can rely on existing code in the `ProcessKeyPress` and `ProcessKeyRelease` methods to figure out how to support input for your four chosen keyboard keys. You can figure out how to use the `MmgBmp` class' methods by researching their use in other parts of the `ScreenGame` class. Perform a text search to figure out how to use the class' methods. You can add more class fields, if need be, to help manage the movement and positioning of your image.

Challenge Solution

A simple solution to this coding challenge requires you only to make adjustments to the keyboard input handlers: the `ProcessKeyPress` and `ProcessKeyRelease` methods. If the target key for left movement is pressed, decrease the X position of our image by one. If the target key for right movement is pressed, increase the X position by one. Use if statements to check that you don't go out of visual range if you so desire. Make sure to turn movement off when a key is released.

That should take care of the first part of the coding challenge. The next part requires us to make our image visible or invisible depending on the target key pressed. In this case, we check to see when the key is released and in response call our image's `SetIsVisible` method with a Boolean value to show or hide the image. In the next section, we'll begin our discussion of some more advanced topics regarding Java classes.

Advanced Class Topics

Classes are an extremely powerful and important new tool in our coding toolbox. We can now create all manner of classes to use in our games and other Java programs. I wanted to talk about a few high-level, advanced, aspects of OOP. In the next few sections, we'll talk about access, class design, and the static main entry point.

Access

Access in this regard refers to the access modifiers you use to define your classes. In my opinion, it's fine to use the public or default modifier while you're designing your software. The need to make aspects of your classes protected or private will become more pronounced to you as your software matures.

You can always refactor your code and tighten up the design by using more appropriate access modifiers in your class designs. In the next section, we'll explore this concept further as we discuss a few points on class design.

Class Design

Class design refers to the structure of the classes you build. What class fields you use, what methods you define, etc. In general, you should keep your class design simple. Add complexity as you need it or if you expect it. For instance, if you often use the same few lines of code when working with your classes, you might want to move it into a class method.

Similarly, don't go overboard with the functionality you support in the classes you're designing. For instance, if you're adding new functionality in the form of class methods, you should ask yourself whether or not that code belongs in the given class, is your class responsible for it, or is another class. It may turn out a new class is in order to handle the functionality you desire.

Static Main Entry Point

We've covered a lot of material on Java classes, but we haven't talked about how you actually execute a Java program. In order to do so, you must have at least one class that has a static main method that matches a specific method signature. Let's look at the signature of a static main method.

```
public static main(String[] args) { ... }
```

The static main entry point for each of the associated video game project has the same name as the project itself. The copy of the game setup for each coding challenge uses the same approach. When you build a project in the NetBeans IDE, you can configure it to have a default class, with a static main, to run when the program is executed.

To set this value, right-click on your Java project in the NetBeans IDE and select the properties option. From the pop-up window, select the "Run" option from the left-hand side of the window.

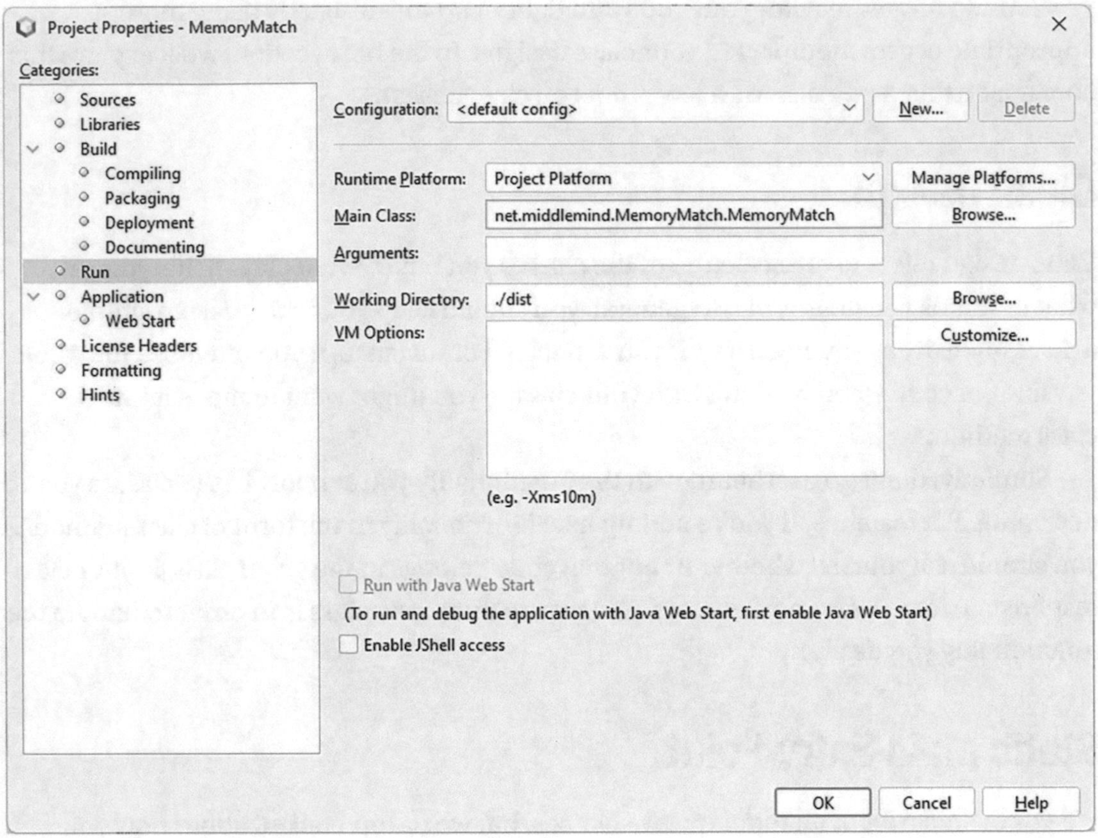

Image 7-1. *Screenshot of a Project's Run Settings in the NetBeans IDE*

A screenshot of the NetBeans IDE's Run settings.

Once you've set the desired static main class, when you build your project, you can execute it by using the following code on the command line. On Windows, you can use a command prompt to execute the commands. On Mac or Linux, you can use a terminal window. Search online for the steps to launch the correct console for your operating system. You can run your newly built Java programs by running a command similar to the following:

```
java -jar MemoryMatch.jar
```

Usually, the newly created JAR file is located in the dist folder of your project's root directory. That would be the best location to run a console command like that shown previously. Before we move on to the next section, a new code challenge, I want to list a very simple class with a static main method.

Listing 7-12. A Basic Java Class with a Static Main Method

```
01 public class SimpleExecutableClass {
02     public int myField = 0;
03
04     public static main(String[] args) {
05         System.out.println("The SimpleExecutableClass has received "
           args.length + " arguments.");
06     }
07 }
```

An example of a simple executable class in Java.

You can use this example as a template for any future executable classes you intend to write. For the most part, you should only have one class with a static main method in your project, but every now and then, you may have more than one. In that case, you can use the following command to specify which static main method you want to run:

```
java -cp MemoryMatch.jar com.test.project.newExecClass
```

If we were testing a new copy of the Memory Match game's main executable, we'd have to run the following command:

```
java -cp MemoryMatch.jar net.middlemind.MemoryMatch.MemoryMatch2
```

In both cases, we're specifying the class to use as the main executable by providing the full class path, package name and class name, as an argument to the -cp command. Think about how the class package factors in here and keep in mind how classes are organized in Java. It'll come in handy when we review libraries in the next chapter. Next up, we'll try another coding challenge and explore static main entry points, project settings, and resources while we're at it.

Challenge: Dungeon Trap's Static Main

In this challenge, the chapter's third and last, we'll take a look at the static main entry point for the Memory Match game. We'll learn a bit more about how a project and its resources are configured, and we'll create a project that has two static main entry points so we can get some experience running select executable classes. Let's take a look at the challenge!

Packages Involved:

```
net.middlemind.MemoryMatch_Chapter7_Challenge3
net.middlemind.MemoryMatch_Chapter7_Challenge3_Solved
```

Description:

Find the package, net.middlemind.MemoryMatch_Chapter7_Challenge3, and open the MemoryMatch.java file. Some of the graphic artists on the project wanted to try out a new set of assets with the Memory Match game but don't want to create a big drain on the developer's time. Your challenge is to create a copy of the MemoryMatch.java static main class and change the game engine configuration file it uses. Point it to this new file instead:

```
engine_config_mmg_memory_match_test.xml
```

This will connect the game to a new set of resources stored in the following directory:

```
.\MemoryMatch\cfg\drawable\MemoryMatchTest
```

You'll need to change the project settings to use the new static main file, run the specific file directly when testing, or use the correct console command to run the new static main executable you just made.

Clue:

Recall from your very first coding challenge where you fixed a version of the Pong Clone game that was accidentally broken after testing. This challenge explored the connection between the Java game project and its resources. Essentially, each game project uses a configuration file that sets the name of the video game and determines which folder to look for game resources.

By creating a new static main for the Memory Match game, you can specify a new game engine configuration file that will in turn specify a new set of resources to use for the game. Take your time to trace through any of the included video game projects to get a better idea of how they are configured.

Challenge Solution

This challenge was an interesting one. In terms of the actual work needed to complete it, it's an easy challenge. However, knowing exactly what to do is not very clear and relies on prior knowledge from previous coding challenges. Let's talk about the steps needed to solve this problem. The first thing you may have noticed is that the challenge asks you to alter the game's configuration file and gives us some new resources to use.

A cursory exploration of the project's directory structure reveals the new configuration file mentioned. Let me point out one important entry in the file:

```
<entry key="NAME" val="MemoryMatchTest" type="string"
from="GameSettings" />
```

This line in the game configuration file is used to find the game's resources in the local configuration folder.

```
./MemoryMatch/cfg/
```

Take a moment to look through the project's cfg directory and keep an eye out for any folders named "MemoryMatchTest". You should have found a folder with that name in the project's drawables resource directory. This folder is marked by its different image resources for the game's logo, board, and countdown numbers.

To solve this challenge, simply copy the static main, MemoryMatch.java, to a new file, MemoryMatchTest.java. Make sure to select the "Refactor Copy" option by right-clicking on the challenge's package and selecting "Paste ➤ Refactor Copy"; specify the correct name, MemoryMatchTest, when refactoring. Now that you have the file set up, you'll want to open it and change the XML configuration file specified in the following class field:

```
public static String ENGINE_CONFIG_FILE = "../cfg/engine_config_mmg_
memory_match_test.xml";
```

Now that you've completed those steps, you should be able to alter the project's settings to use the new static main executable by default. Or you can simply run the target file either in the IDE, by right-clicking it and selecting "Run File", or by using the correct console command. The choice is yours. The main takeaway here is to understand the importance of the static main entry point and to get more experience working with the game engine. You should see the version of the game with grayscale images for a few key resources as opposed to color images (Image 7-2).

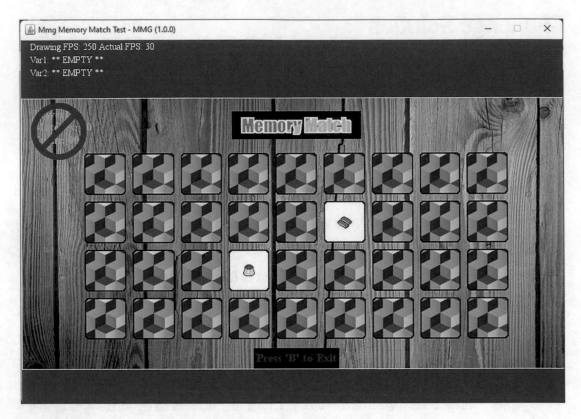

Image 7-2. *Screenshot of the Modified Memory Match Clone*

A set of screenshots showing the cloned version of the Memory Match game with altered configuration file that points to an alternate game resource folder with some grayscale resources replacing color images.

That brings us to the conclusion of this section. Take your time and work through the chapter's code challenges with care. If you get stuck, use the solution package to figure out where you went wrong.

Conclusion

That brings us to the conclusion of the first chapter on Java classes. In this chapter, we took the time to talk about some of the OOP of the Java programming language. We even took the time to explore some subtle points of class design and took on three coding challenges. Not too shabby. Let's take a look at a summary of the material we've covered here.

What We Covered

Let's take a look at the object-oriented programming topics and coding challenges we encountered in this chapter:

- Class Declarations: We took a look at some basic class definitions and talked about access modifiers at this level.

- Fields: We discussed adding fields to our classes and using access modifiers to control how those class fields are used.

- Methods: We furthered our exploration of Java classes by reviewing class methods, access modifiers, method parameters, and more.

- Static Members: We managed to refine our understanding of classes further by reviewing static class members like static fields and methods.

- Constructors: Class initialization never got easier. We took a look at class constructors and differentiated between default and custom constructors.

- Challenge: The MmgBmp Class: This challenge gave us some direct experience modifying a game by adding our own image to it. We got some more experience working with game engine classes like MmgBmp and ScreenGame. We also got to add our own image to the game screen!

- Challenge: The ScreenGame Class: This challenge gave us more experience with user input. We got to configure the ScreenGame class to handle new keyboard input to animate, show, and hide our new game image. In this way, we added a little unnecessary game feature, but it's the same process when adding similar new game features.

- Access: A slightly more advanced topic; we discussed some finer points about access modifiers in our classes.

- Class Design: We discussed some class design concepts. Higher-level ideas that you should have in mind when designing your classes.

- Static Main Entry Point: A very important topic; you can't run your programs without a static main entry point. We covered this topic and demonstrated how to create a static main class and how to execute both a package default and a target executable Java class.

- Challenge: Dungeon Trap's Static Main: The last challenge in the chapter; we got more experience with the game engine, game engine configuration files, game resources, and static main entry points by creating a new executable Java class for the Memory Match game that uses a different set of game resources.

Java classes are an extremely powerful tool to add to our coding toolbox. You will use classes every time you sit down and write a Java program. Knowing how to create classes and define their use via access modifiers, custom constructors, and class methods opens up a whole universe of new possibilities for you as a Java developer. In the next chapter, we'll take things even further as we review some powerful language features that let us use classes in even more ways.

CHAPTER 8

Encapsulation, Inheritance, and Polymorphism

This chapter is all about advanced Java OOP topics like encapsulation, inheritance, and polymorphism. Together they constitute three of the four main theoretical principles of object-oriented programming. The fourth principle, abstraction, is beyond the scope of this text, so we won't be covering it here. Let's set the stage for the discussion by defining each of these features of the Java, object-oriented, programming language.

- Encapsulation: The *process of wrapping code and data together into a single unit* usually expressed as a Java class with highly controlled field access via class methods.

- Inheritance: A key feature of OOP that allows us to create a new class from an existing class. The new class that is created is known as the subclass (child or derived class), and the existing class, from which the child class is derived, is known as a super-class (parent or base class).

- Polymorphism: Polymorphism works with inheritance by allowing us to use inherited class methods differently than the super-class' implementation.

We'll take a close look at each of these advanced topics in turn as we complete our review of Java's object-oriented programming support, and we'll get to work with a new game as we do it: Dungeon Trap! Enjoy!

© Victor G. Brusca 2023
V. G. Brusca, *Introduction to Java Through Game Development*, https://doi.org/10.1007/978-1-4842-8951-8_8

Encapsulation

Encapsulation is the first principle of object-oriented programming that we'll explore.
Encapsulation in Java refers to the strategic protection of data, class fields, through the
use of access modifiers and class methods. Let's motivate the review with an example of
basic encapsulation in a Java class.

Listing 8-1. Example of Encapsulation in a Simple Java Class

```
01 public class BasicEncapClass {
02     private int field1 = 0;
03
04     public BasicEncapClass(int i) {
05         this.field1 = i;
06     }
07
08     public int getField1() {
09         return this.field1;
10     }
11
12     public void setField1(int i) {
13         this.field1 = i;
14     }
15 }
```

An example of a simple Java class employing basic encapsulation.

***Java Programming Note: I like to take the notion of encapsulation a bit further
than just the protection of class data with get and set methods. I like to think
of proper encapsulation as also including the proper exposure of complex class
functionality through a simple set of class methods.*

In a well-encapsulated class, by definition, we protect access to the class fields by
making them private. Then open up controlled access to said fields by using get and
set methods. I know it's a little bit anticlimactic. The actual implementation of this

OOP philosophy is not difficult at all. In my opinion, you can over-encapsulate when designing a game or other Java program. And you can add some unnecessary extra overhead to your game if you do.

For instance, should all your simple game classes use strict encapsulation? This would make all field access to those classes require a method call, and method calls are, in most cases, less efficient than a direct public field access. There's not much more to discuss on the topic. It boils down to applying strict control of class fields using a class' get and set methods and field access modifiers. In the next section, we'll discuss class inheritance in Java and discover how to create classes based on other, existing, classes.

Inheritance

Inheritance, in Java, is one of the key features of OOP that allows us to create a new class from an existing class. The new class that is created is known as a subclass, and the existing class from where the child class is derived is known as the super-class. Let's see how we can actually declare a subclass in Java. We're going to build off of the class we used in Listing 8-1. Keep an eye out for how encapsulation and inheritance work together.

Listing 8-2. Example of Encapsulation and Inheritance Using Java Classes

```
//class declarations
01 public class BasicEncapClass {
02     private int field1 = 0;
03
04     public BasicEncapClass(int i) {
05         this.field1 = i;
06     }
07
08     public int getField1() {
09         return this.field1;
10     }
11
12     public void setField1(int i) {
13         this.field1 = i;
14     }
15 }
```

```
16
17 public class BasicSubClass extends BasicEncapClass {
18     private int newField1 = 1;
19
20     public BasicSubClass(int i) {
21         super(i);
22         this.newField1 = i;
23     }
24
25     @Override
26     public int getField1() {
27         return this.newField1;
28     }
29
30     @Override
31     public void setField1(int i) {
32         this.newField1 = i;
33     }
34 }
```

An example of a set of simple Java classes using encapsulation and inheritance.

Notice the use of inheritance in the example classes in Listing 8-2. The class BasicSubClass extends the class BasicEncapClass. You can declare a new subclass using the extends keyword. You can only have one super-class in Java, meaning you can only extend one other class at a time. In this example, the subclass declares a new class field, constructor, and get/set methods. In the new constructor, there is a special keyword I want you to take a look at, super, on line 21.

The super keyword allows you to access the super-class of the current class to call available methods and access available fields. It has another use in the case of the subclass constructor. The first line in the constructor, and only the first line, can call a super-class constructor. In this case, when you create a new instance of the BasicSubClass class, it will call the constructor of the BasicEncapClass. Also, note that the subclass keeps the same methods, getField1 and setField1, except that it redefines their functionality to work with a new class field.

The @Override keyword is a special method annotation that indicates the current method overrides, replaces, a super-class method of the same name. Did you see how encapsulation and inheritance work together in Java OOP programming? By hiding class fields and exposing functionality via class methods, subclasses can maintain and extend the functionality of their super-classes in a controlled way. In the next section, we'll take on a coding challenge that incorporates our new knowledge of Java OOP programming.

Challenge: Inheritance

In this coding challenge, the chapter's first, you'll have to rely on your knowledge of class inheritance to add a new weapon to the Dungeon Trap game. Let's jump into a coding challenge!

Packages Involved:

```
net.middlemind.DungeonTrap_Chapter8_Challenge1
net.middlemind.DungeonTrap_Chapter8_Challenge1_Solved
```

Description:

Find the package, net.middlemind.DungeonTrap_Chapter8_Challenge1, and open the MdtWeaponSpear.java file. You've been tasked with completing some work on the Dungeon Trap game. The task you've been given is to explore adding a flame spear to the game as the default weapon for both players. The graphics for the new weapon asset can be found in the game project's image resources directory:

```
./cfg/drawable/DungeonTrap
```

You also must plug the new weapon into the game. Since there is already a spear weapon in the game, the lead programmer has asked you to use inheritance to create the new Java class. Keep everything the same except the images used and make the new weapon more powerful and slightly slower. Make sure the weapon is the default weapon for both players. This will require changing the MdtCharInter.java class, the super-class for player and enemy characters in the game. You must run this package's file – DungeonTrap.java; right-click and select Run File to test the game.

Clue:

If you get stuck, take a close look at how the MdtWeaponSpear.java class is used in the MdtCharInter.java class. If you change the images and attack properties of the default spear, you can make it look and act like a flame spear. Think about that. Then think about inheritance in Java and using copy and paste to create a quick copy of an existing class. One last hint, the default weapon for players and enemies is set in the constructor of the MdtCharInter.java class.

Challenge Solution

This challenge is one of the more advanced ones in the text, but if you carefully read through the description and the clue, I think there's enough information there for you to get it. The entire solution really rests on your use of Java inheritance. The goal here is to use an existing weapon class, the MdtWeaponSpear.java, to create a new version of the spear. There are four adjustments to the code, including the creation of the new flame spear Java weapon class, you must make in order to add the new weapon to the game as the default player weapon. Let's go through them in detail now.

As we mentioned earlier, the first adjustment you have to make is to refactor copy the MdtWeaponSpear.java class and rename to something that resembles a flame spear class. We chose to call it the MdtWeaponSpearFlame.java class. Next, we have to alter the image resources used to display the weapon so that it looks more like a flame spear and less like a regular spear. The image assets are already included for you in the game's resource folder.

Find them and use the name of the image files, including the extension to change the image resources used by the new flame spear class. Next, we were asked to make the weapon perform differently, a stronger but slower attack. To this end, we increased the attack strength from 1 point to 2 and slowed the weapon down by 100ms by decreasing the weapon time from 250ms to 350ms.

Lastly, we need to set the flame spear as the default weapon for all players in the game. To accomplish this, we have to look at the MdtCharInter.java class. This is the super-class for all characters in the game and as such has the code that sets the default weapon. Follow the example set by the existing code to add the new weapon to the list of the character's supported weapons and then set it as the equipped weapon. If you make all the appropriate adjustments, you should end up with a red spear like the one shown in Image 8-1.

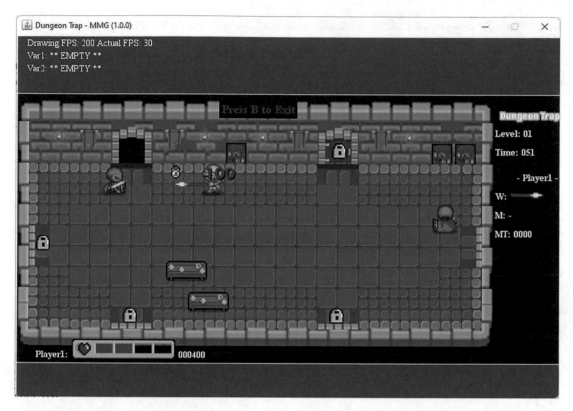

Image 8-1. *A Screenshot Showing the New Flame Spear in Action*

A screenshot depicting the new flame spear in action in the Dungeon Trap game.

That brings us to the conclusion of this section of the chapter. We'll pick things back up in our review of advanced class topics with a discussion on polymorphism in Java. If you could not get your coding changes to work properly for this challenge, take a moment to review the solution package's code.

Polymorphism

Polymorphism, defined outside of the context of computer programming, means "many forms," and it occurs when we have classes that are related to one another by inheritance. In fact, we've seen an example of it earlier in this chapter; we just didn't know it yet. Let me present to you the same listing we looked at earlier, Listing 8-2, which we'll now discuss with regard to polymorphism in Java OO programming.

Listing 8-3. Example of Encapsulation, Inheritance, and Polymorphism Using
Java Classes

```
//class declarations
01 public class BasicEncapClass {
02      private int field1 = 0;
03
04      public BasicEncapClass(int i) {
05          this.field1 = i;
06      }
07
08      public int getField1() {
09          return this.field1;
10      }
11
12      public void setField1(int i) {
13          this.field1 = i;
14      }
15 }
16
17 public class BasicSubClass extends BasicEncapClass {
18      private int newField1 = 1;
19
20      public BasicSubClass(int i) {
21              super(i);
22          this.newField1 = i;
23      }
24
25      @Override
26      public int getField1() {
27          return this.newField1;
28      }
29
30      @Override
31      public void setField1(int i) {
32          this.newField1 = i;
```

```
33      }
34 }
```

An example listing, the same as Listing 8-2, which demonstrates basic inheritance and polymorphism. Notice how encapsulation factors into the super-class definition.

What? We're looking at the same class listing but using it to review a different topic. What gives? Well, I used the same listing for a reason. I wanted you to notice that the concepts of encapsulation, inheritance, and polymorphism go hand in hand and are closely tied to one another. Without a well-encapsulated class, inheritance becomes less useful and almost chaotic, relying on class fields and access modifiers to control usage.

With good encapsulation comes good inheritance, and that brings us to polymorphism. Take a moment to look over the two overridden methods, getField1 and setField1, on lines 26 and 31 respectively. Methods with the same names exist in the BasicEncapClass but are now being redefined in the BasicSubClass class. This is an example of polymorphism as the name of the method stays static, but its meaning and usage can change.

This topic can be a bit confusing and seem almost circular in some ways, so let's take a moment to look at it from a slightly different angle. Instead of using meaningless, fictional classes, let's try to demonstrate these programming features using classes and concepts we're more familiar with: fish. Let's look at some code!

Listing 8-4. Example of Encapsulation, Inheritance, and Polymorphism by Modeling Fish

```
//class declarations
01 class Fish {
02      private int avgLen;
03      private int avgWeight;
04      private String color;
05
06      public Fish() {
07      }
08
09      public int getAvgLen() {
10          return this.avgLen;
11      }
12
```

```
13      public void setAvgLen(int i) {
14          this.avgLen = i;
15      }
16
17      public int getAvgWeight() {
18          return this.avgWeight;
19      }
20
21      public void setAvgWeight(int i) {
22          this.avgWeight = i;
23      }
24
25      public String getColor() {
26          return this.color;
27      }
28
29      public void setColor(String s) {
30          this.color = s;
31      }
32
33      public String getName() {
34          return "Fish";
35      }
36
37      public String getFoodSource() {
38          return "Worms";
39      }
40
41      @Override
42      public String toString() {
43          return "This fish, " + this.getName() + ", eats '" + this.
            getFoodSource() + "'.";
44      }
45  }
46
```

```
47 class Trout extends Fish {
48     public Trout() {
49         super.setAvgLen(25);
50         super.setAvgWeight(8);
51         super.setColor("Brown");
52     }
53
54     @Override
55     public String getName() {
56         return "Trout";
57     }
58
59     @Override
60     public String getFoodSource() {
61         return "Worms and insects";
62     }
63 }
64
65 class RainbowTrout extends Trout {
66     public RainbowTrout() {
67         super.setAvgLen(30);
68         super.setAvgWeight(10);
69         super.setColor("Rainbow");
70     }
71
72     @Override
73     public String getName() {
74         return "Rainbow Trout";
75     }
76 }

//code
01 Fish fish = new Fish();
02 System.out.println("fish - toString: " + fish);
03 System.out.println("");
04
```

```
05 Trout trout = new Trout();
06 System.out.println("trout - toString: " + trout);
07 fish = trout;
08 System.out.println("fish = trout - toString: " + fish);
09 System.out.println("");
10
11 RainbowTrout rbTrout = new RainbowTrout();
12 System.out.println("rbTrout - toString: " + rbTrout);
13 trout = (Trout)rbTrout;
14 System.out.println("trout = rbTrout - toString: " + trout);
15 fish = (Fish)trout;
16 System.out.println("fish = trout - toString: " + fish);
17 fish = (Fish)rbTrout;
18 System.out.println("fish = rbTrout - toString: " + fish);

//output
01 //fish
02 fish - toString: This fish, Fish, eats 'Worms'.
03
04 //trout
05 trout - toString: This fish, Trout, eats 'Worms and insects'.
06 fish = trout - toString: This fish, Trout, eats 'Worms and insects'.
07
08 //rainbow trout
09 rbTrout - toString: This fish, Rainbow Trout, eats 'Worms and insects'.
10 trout = rbTrout - toString: This fish, Rainbow Trout, eats 'Worms and
   insects'.
11 fish = trout - toString: This fish, Rainbow Trout, eats 'Worms and
   insects'.
12 fish = rbTrout - toString: This fish, Rainbow Trout, eats 'Worms and
   insects'.
```

An example of a properly encapsulated class, Fish, extended by the Trout class, which is extended by the RainbowTrout class. Notice that each extended class is also an instance of its super-class. Certain classes override method behavior in a demonstration of polymorphism.

**Game Programming Note: Class inheritance is a very powerful tool to use when designing the class structure of your game. Quite often in games, you'll have enemies, weapons, and items that are more specific instances of a general classification. Class inheritance works very well when modeling this structure.*

Listing 8-4 is a rather long one; take your time to read over it carefully before moving on. This example shows the three key aspects of OO programming we've covered here all working in tandem. Let's review what's going on and cover some finer points as we do so. First of all, the Fish class is an example of a well-encapsulated class. It has three fields – avgWeight, avgLen, and color. It also defines two methods that provide specific information about the fish: the getName and getFoodSource methods.

The last method in the class needs a bit of explanation. The toString method is prefixed with the override annotation, which indicates that it replaces an existing method. But which one? We haven't defined a toString method. Well, it turns out in Java, as we've mentioned before, that every class is a subclass of the Object super-class, and this super-class defines a toString method that provides a string representation of the class.

By overriding it, we are customizing the method to return a specific value. In this case, the following statement:

This fish, [fish name], eats '[food source]'

This is an example of polymorphism as the toString method has now been redefined specifically for the Fish class. In the next example, the Trout class, a trout being a specific type of fish, extends the Fish class. The class definition relies on inheritance to extend the super-class, Fish, and polymorphism to redefine certain super-class methods. In this case, the Trout class redefines the getName and getFoodSource methods to provide a trout-specific implementation.

To motivate the example further, a third class, RainbowTrout, is defined, which extends the Trout class. This class, being a specific type of trout, only has to customize some class methods, already defined from the Trout and the Fish class. In this case, all we have to do is override the getName method to specify the class is a rainbow trout class. Notice that each class that extends the Fish class, or a subclass of the Fish class, inherits its overridden toString method.

Take a look at the output text provided and trace how each class instance is being cast up to its super-class: the Fish class. Notice that the output remains customized even though we're interacting with the object as an instance of a Fish class. This is an example of polymorphism as the class is an instance of itself and all of its super-classes. It also exemplifies method polymorphism in Java.

The @override method annotation is used to indicate that a method is a replacement for a method defined by a super-class. In this way, new, custom, functionality can be defined, on a method-by-method basis, for the inheriting class. This allows inheriting classes to extend super-class functionality. Polymorphism in Java not only applies to the overriding of class methods to customize functionality, it also applies to the fact that subclasses are also an instance of their super-class.

In this way, an instance of the Trout class is also an instance of the Fish class, which is also an instance of the Object class and so on. This aspect of polymorphism is demonstrated in the casting of subclasses to super-classes on lines 13–17. In the next section, we'll take a look at a coding challenge involving polymorphism and the Dungeon Trap game.

Challenge: Polymorphism

The second coding challenge for this chapter will test your ability to leverage Java's polymorphic capabilities to change how the flame spear you implemented in the previous challenge functions in the game. This is the third challenge in the text that starts off from the solution to the previous challenge. As such, it's vitally important that you have the correct solution to the previous challenge before proceeding. Take a moment to double-check and make sure. As always, enjoy the challenge!

Packages Involved:

```
net.middlemind.DungeonTrap_Chapter8_Challenge2
net.middlemind.DungeonTrap_Chapter8_Challenge2_Solved
```

Description:

Find the package, net.middlemind.DungeonTrap_Chapter8_Challenge2, and open the MdtWeaponSpearFlame.java file. This challenge is another of the more complicated challenges, and as such, you'll need to look at code in the following Java classes:

- MdtWeaponSpearFlame.java

- MdtWeapon.java

- ScreenGame.java

- MdtWeaponAxe.java

Some of the developers like the new spear but think it's too similar to the original spear. They want to test out making the spear shoot out, like a throwing weapon, instead. In order to implement this change, you'll need to make a few adjustments to the code. There's a weapon that exists as a throwing weapon, the MdtWeaponAxe.java class. There are a few methods that we need to use from this class to make our weapon throwable. First, you'll need to copy and paste the following methods from the MdtWeaponAxe.java file to the MdtWeaponSpearFlame.java file:

- GetX()

- SetX(int i)

- GetY()

- SetY(int i)

- SetPosition(MmgVector2 v)

- SetPosition(int x, int y)

This will allow the new flame spear to handle setting its X, Y coordinate or position in the same way the axe, a throwable weapon, does. Next, we'll need to adjust the super-class of all weapons, the MdtWeapon.java class, to support the new throwable spear. Find the following methods in this class:

- GetWeaponRect()

- MmgDraw(MmgPen p)

There are special branches of code to handle a throwing axe; expand the two if statements to support throwable spears as well. A similar change must be made to the ScreenGame.java class' `ProcessAClick` method. Find the two places in the method where you have to alter an if statement to include throwable spears, not just axes. Making these adjustments will make the new spear fly out and rotate, if implemented properly. You must run this package's file – DungeonTrap.java; right-click and select Run File to test the game.

Clue:

This is a tough challenge, and there's not much in the way of a clue to guide you if you run into trouble. Carefully read through the classes and methods provided in the description. Keep an eye out for the different behavior of the axe in the code and keep in mind you're making a throwing spear, so it will function the same way as the axe.

Challenge Solution

The solution to this challenge, as we mentioned earlier, requires the correct solution to this chapter's first challenge on inheritance. If you ran into trouble but want to keep moving forward, you can use the solution to challenge 1 in Chapter 7 as the starting point for this challenge by copying and pasting in the marked code changes. This solution requires you to make five changes to the game's code in order to successfully solve the challenge.

This solution requires making changes in five different places. Let me list the locations of the adjustments and the order we've assigned them. You could have done things in a different way, and that's just fine.

- MdtWeaponSpearFlame.java and MdtWeaponAxe.java: In this case, we need to copy the methods that override positioning functionality, allowing the weapon to move independently of the wielder.

- MdtWeapon.java: An adjustment is necessary in the `GetWeaponRect` method.

- MdtWeapon.java: An adjustment is necessary in `MmgDraw` method.

- ScreenGame.java: An adjustment is necessary in the `ProcessAClick` when firing the weapon.

Let's review the adjustment made in sequence and in some details. The first change that we need to make uses polymorphism to override the functionality of the super-class positioning methods. The adjustment we're making here allows the weapon to now move independently of the player holding it. We can get away with reusing the code from the `MdtWeaponAxe` class because it is also throwable. Next, we move on to the MdtWeapon.java class and take a look at the `GetWeaponRect` method. This method is used to calculate the rectangle that describes where the weapon should be drawn on the screen.

For stabbing weapons that aren't thrown, the method calculates the rectangle based on how far into the stab animation the weapon is. For thrown weapons, the axe and now the flame spear, we return the rectangle that describes where the projectile is on the screen and what direction it's facing. The if statements need to be adjusted to include the SPEAR weapon type. You have all the tools you need in your coding toolbox to get it done. A similar change needs to be made to the MmgDraw method to include the spear when drawing thrown weapons.

Notice that this class, MdtWeapon, is the super-class of the MdtWeaponAxe, MdtWeaponSpear, and MdtWeaponSpearFlame classes. That's why changing the code here affects all extended classes. The centralization gives us leverage but also increases complexity as we have to support different weapons, throwing and stabbing, at this level. The last change we need to make is to support adding a new copy of the weapon to the game's drawable objects. This is accomplished in the ScreenGame class' ProcessAClick method. When the player fires the weapon, a clone of it is added to the game. Because of all the changes we've made, this clone can fly off on its own and rotate while doing so until it collides with something.

Those are the changes we needed to make to solve this coding challenge. Not an easy task by any means and it definitely took a few tools from our coding toolbox to do it. Don't worry if you didn't get it; as long as you learn by reviewing the solution, you're doing a great job. In the next section, we'll wrap up our review of classes by talking about how to share them and include them in our programs.

Importing Class Libraries

Now that you have a good understanding of Java classes and OOP concepts like encapsulation, inheritance, and polymorphism, you need to develop a good understanding of how to package up your code and use it in other programs. To do this, you'll need to build a Java project and get the resulting JAR file. In most cases, these types of projects do not contain a static main method and only contain Java classes.

This is commonly referred to as a library. You can share your libraries by sharing your project's JAR file. To add a library to a project in the NetBeans IDE, right-click on a project and select "Properties" from the context menu. In the properties popup, select the "Libraries" option from the left-hand categories section. When using a local JAR file, we'll add a new entry to the "classpath" section. Click the "+" button and select "Add JAR/Folder" from the available options. A screenshot of this process is shown in Image 8-2.

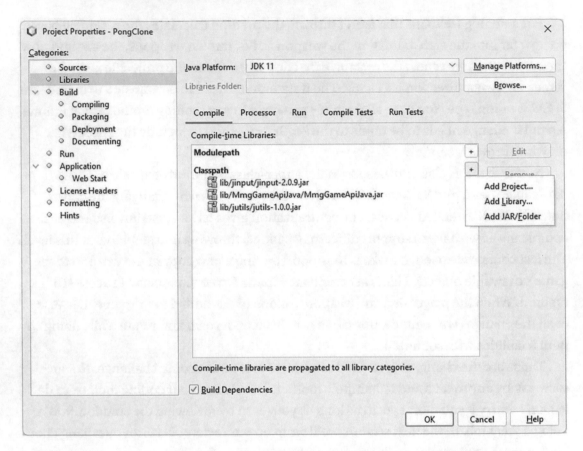

Image 8-2. *Screenshot of a Project's Libraries Settings in the NetBeans IDE*

A screenshot showing the "Libraries" section of the project's properties popup.

This process is the same process you used in Chapter 1 to set up the video game project with their local library files. Now that you have a library added to your project, you'll need to include that package in your Java program before you can use it. To do so, you use Java's `import` keyword. An example of importing the video game engine's main packages is as follows:

```
import net.middlemind.MmgGameApiJava.MmgCore.*;
import net.middlemind.MmgGameApiJava.MmgBase.*;
```

When using the wildcard feature of the class import process, you will get access to all classes in the specified Java package. This is convenient but isn't intuitive, and it hides which classes actually belong to which packages. Let's take a look at how to import just one Java class. In this case, we're adding access to the `MmgBmp` class.

```
import net.middlemind.MmgGameApiJava.MmgCore.MmgBmp;
```

Notice that all Java classes are imported by their package name. Keep this in mind as you work with Java. Take the time to get to know the most commonly used packages in Java's included framework of classes. Two important ones that you'll use quite often are `java.io` and `java.util`. You can find out more about the classes available in the Java framework at this address:

```
https://docs.oracle.com/en/java/javase/11/docs/api/index.html
```

That brings us to the conclusion of this section on importing and accessing libraries of classes. In the next section, we'll take a look at the general, shared, structure of the video game projects.

Video Game Project Structure

Because all of the included video game projects are based on the same game engine, they share a similar setup and configuration. The following three Java classes set up the static main entry point and two key classes that plug the game engine's screen into a window and panel. I'll list the classes here:

Game's Static Main Entry Point: Usually named after the game itself, PongClone. java, MemoryMatch.java, and DungeonTrap.java. This part of the project provides the executable class for the game. It also, as you've seen in a few coding challenges, sets up the connection between the video game and its resources via the game engine's config file.

MainFrame.java: This class sets up the window of main frame where the `GamePanel` class will render itself. This class is mainly set up to maintain the super-class functionality. Note that it inherits from the game engine's library of classes.

GamePanel.java: This class is responsible for handling events from the loading and splash screens and for switching between game screens depending on the game state. Much of the functionality of this class comes from its super-class.

Using these three classes with minor adjustments, refactoring the executable class and pointing the game to a new game engine configuration file, is the basis for setting up a new game. A very important class field in the game's executable class is the `ENGINE_CONFIG_FILE`. I've listed the class field from the Pong Clone game.

```
/**
 * Base engine config files.
 */
public static String ENGINE_CONFIG_FILE = "../cfg/engine_config_mmg_
pong_clone.xml";
```

The game engine configuration file is used to specify a few key game engine settings. The main one we need to worry about is the NAME entry. The file uses an XML encoding, but it should be simple enough for you to edit without any research. Simply change the value in the "val" attribute of the name entry. This value has to be the same name as the folder that contains the game's resources.

```
<entry key="NAME" val="MemoryMatch" type="string"
from="GameSettings" />
```

which corresponds to the following directory structure local to the NetBeans project folder:

```
./cfg
-> class_config
   -> MemoryMatch
-> drawable
   -> MemoryMatch
   -> MemoryMatchTest
-> playable
   -> MemoryMatch
-> engine_config_mmg_memory_match.xml
-> engine_config_mmg_memory_match_test.xml
```

Some aspects of the game engine are beyond the scope of this text, but I want you to be able to create a new game and a video game project using the game engine. There are four supported resources in the cfg folder. The class_config directory contains configuration files used to adjust resources in a given game's specific classes. The entries in this file provide data at runtime to set up a game screen's image resources among other things.

The drawable directory is used to hold image resources, and the following image file types are supports: PNG and JPG. Any image placed in the game's folder will be loaded automatically and accessible by its full file name, including extension. We've also seen the image loading process before from previous coding challenges. The playable directory is similar to the drawable directory except that it is used to load sound files. We recommend using WAV files for your sound effects and music.

Lastly, there are a few XML files in the base of the cfg folder. These are the game engine config files for specific copies of the game. Multiple projects can point to the same resources. This is exemplified in how the coding challenges are set up. Each challenge is a package in the game project itself and is configured, for the most part, to access the same resource and configuration files. You'll notice that there is an auto_load folder in the drawable and playable directories. Any resources found in these folders are loaded by default and available to you in your game by its full file name.

That brings us to the conclusion of this section on configuration and setup of the video game projects included with the text. In the next section, you'll be challenged to create a new video game project on your own. Enjoy!

Challenge: Create a New Game Project

In this, the third challenge of the chapter, we'll explore setting up a new game project. There's not much more to it than that. This is a tough challenge; you may not make it through on your first try; don't worry. You can always reference an existing project to see how it's set up and copy the configuration.

Projects Involved:

PongClone
MyNewGameSolved

Description:

This challenge is all about you. We won't be doing any development tasks for anyone or anything like that. In this challenge, you're going to explore the configuration of the video game project by creating a new game project that is a functioning clone of an existing project. I should mention that this is the first challenge where the solution is a project and not a package.

Your goal is to use your knowledge about the NetBeans IDE, the game engine, and the project configuration from all the preceding chapters to clone the Pong Clone game into a new project named "MyNewGame". I'll outline the general steps needed to solve this challenge and leave it up to you. We'll review the process in detail in this challenge's solution section.

1. Create a new NetBeans IDE project with the name "MyNewGame".

2. Add and configure the library files for jutils, jinput, and the MmgGameApiJava libraries.

3. Copy the PongClone project's cfg directory to the local directory of the new MyNewGame project.

4. Copy all the Java class files from the PongClone project's net. middlemind.PongClone package and "refactor copy" them into the new project. Name the refactored package whatever you would like.

5. Configure the project's settings including the default static main class, the output directory, the Java version, and the working directory.

6. Execute the project and verify that the Pong Clone game runs correctly.

Give it your best shot, good luck!

Clue:

You can use any of the associated video game projects as an example of how to configure your new NetBeans project. Use the PongClone project as an example of the actual classes and game resources to use. Remember, you want to create a copy of the Pong Clone game as a starting point for a new video game by cloning it into a new NetBeans project.

Challenge Solution

The solution to this challenge isn't obvious. You have to work through a number of configuration steps in order to create new video game project with a functioning copy of the Pong Clone game as the seed configuration of the project. Let's go over each step in the process in detail.

Step 1: Create a New Project to Customize

Select "File ➤ New Project" from the NetBeans menu. Choose "Java Application" for the project type.

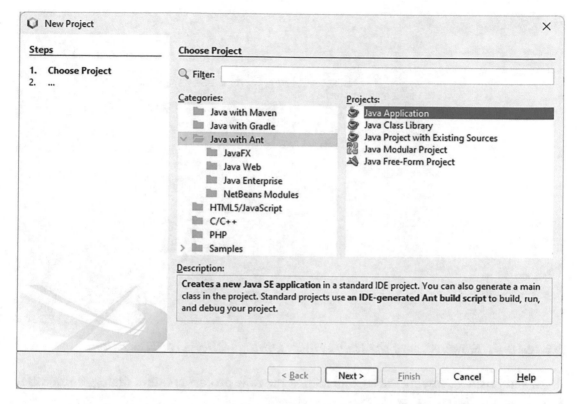

Image 8-3. *Screenshot of the New Project Dialog – Choose Project Type*

Select the Java Application option from the Java with Ant project category.

Set the "Project Name" to "MyNewGame" and select the location of the project. Don't select the Create Main Class option as we'll use a copy of one from the PongClone project.

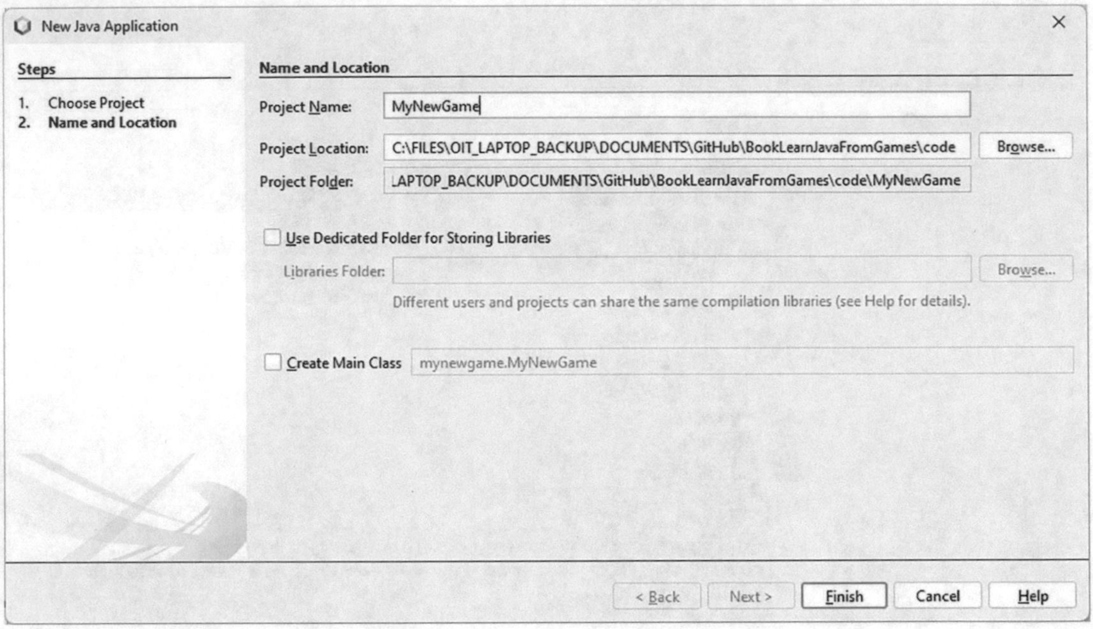

Image 8-4. *Screenshot of the New Project Dialog – Name and Location*

A screenshot showing the second step in the new project creation dialog. Remember NOT to check the Create Main Class checkbox.

Complete the project creation process and expand its entry in the NetBeans project list.

Step 2: Add the Default Project Libraries

Once the new project is set up, now you have to configure the base set of libraries like we did in Chapter 1. Feel free to refer back in to review the process in order to complete this step. A screenshot showing the added Java libraries is shown in Image 8-5.

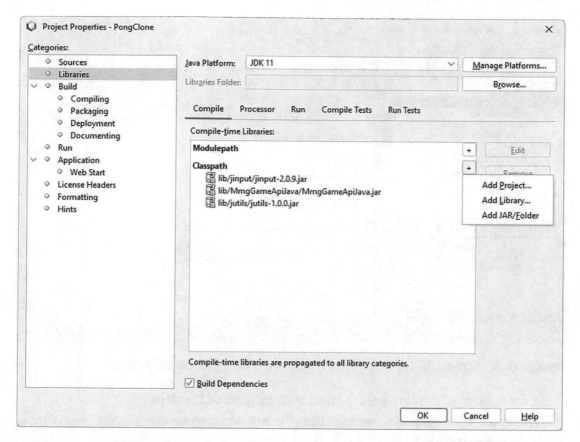

Image 8-5. *Screenshot of the Project's Properties with Configured Libraries*

A screenshot showing the MyNewGame project with configured set of base libraries. Use Chapter 1 as a reference on how to set up the project's libraries.

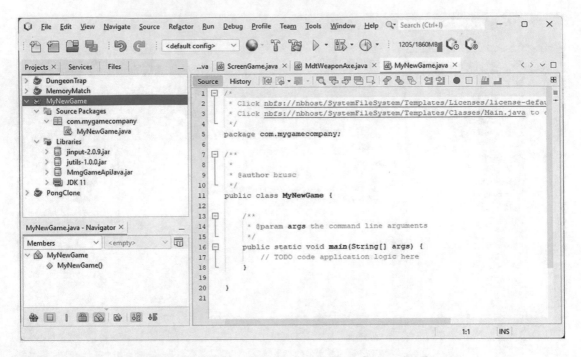

Image 8-6. *Screenshot of the New Project with Configured Libraries*

A screenshot of the new game project with configured libraries.

The new NetBeans project and the libraries are set up so we can add the Pong Clone game's resource folder.

Step 3: Copy Over the Resource Folder

The resource folder, cfg, is located on the root directory of each game's NetBeans project folder. It contains all the game resources and configuration information. Copying it to a new project makes it available as a source of game resources and configuration information for the new project.

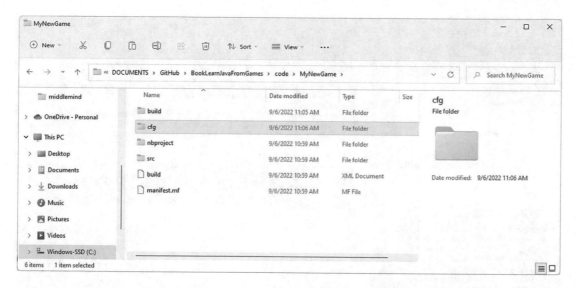

Image 8-7. *Screenshot of the New Project with Game Resource Folder – cfg*

A screenshot showing the new game project with the copied-over configuration and resource folder, cfg.

Simply copy and paste the folder from the Pong Clone game's project folder into the new game's project folder. We'll want to customize the game's configuration file a little so that we can tell it's a different version of the game. Find and open the game's XML configuration file located here:

```
./MyNewGame/cfg/ engine_config_mmg_pong_clone.xml
```

We want to change the TITLE and COMPANY_NAME entries to new string values so we can tell our version of the game apart.

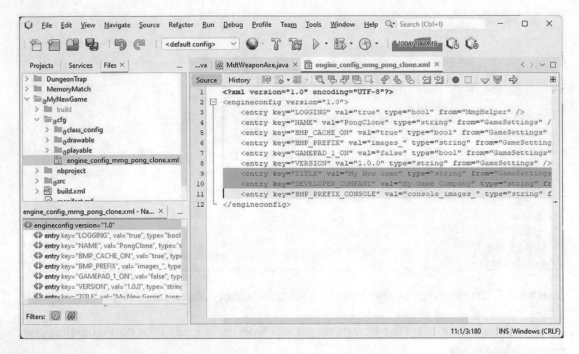

Image 8-8. *Screenshot of the New Project's engine_config_mmg_pong_clone Config File*

A screenshot of the new game project's game engine configuration file with TITLE and COMPANY_NAME entries changed to indicate a new copy of the game.

You can open and edit the file right in the NetBeans IDE by locating it in the "Files" tab. Expand the entry for the new game project and locate the file in the cfg directory.

Step 4: Copy Over the PongClone Java Classes

We'll populate our new project with Java classes from the Pong Clone game. You can copy and paste them from project to project directly in the NetBeans IDE.

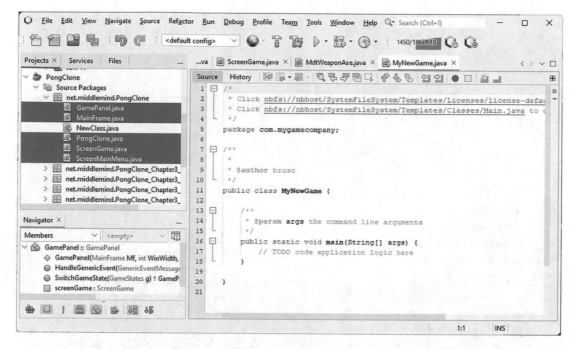

Image 8-9. *Screenshot Showing the Selection of the Pong Clone Class Files*

A screenshot showing the selection of the PongClone project's Java class files.

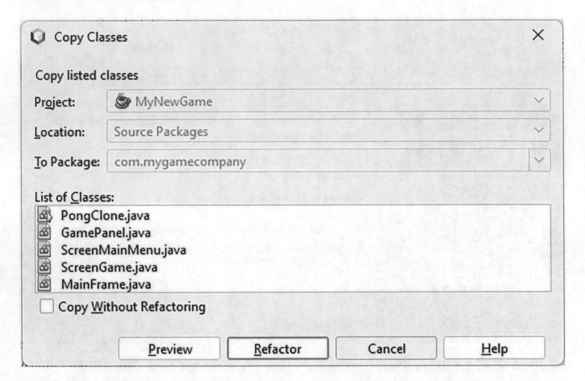

Image 8-10. *Screenshot Showing the Refactor Copy Dialog*

A screenshot showing the refactor copy dialog. Click the refactor button to refactor copy the classes into the new game project.

You should rename the main executable class from "PongClone.java" to "MyNewGame.java" by right-clicking the file and selecting "Refactor ➤ Rename" from the context menu, as shown in Image 8-11.

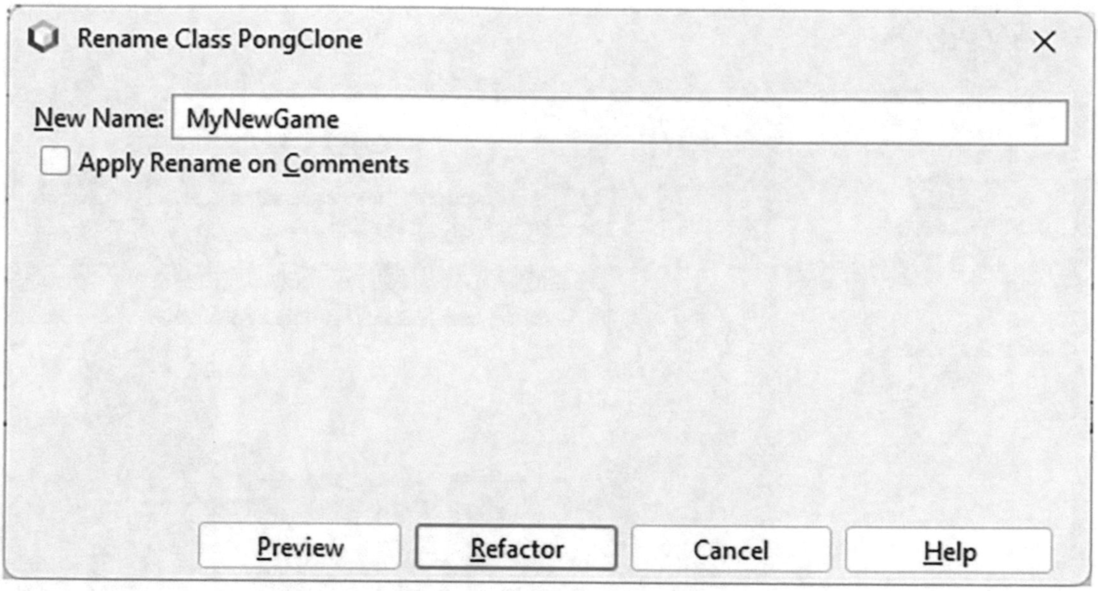

Image 8-11. *Screenshot Showing the Renaming of the PongClone Main Class*

A screenshot showing the rename file refactoring dialog.

You're almost ready to run the game. You have the classes copied into place, the libraries set up, and you've plugged in the resource folder. Next up, we'll fine-tune some project settings.

Step 5: Configure Project Settings

There are a few project settings you should see to before running the game. The first is to set the "Working Directory" for the project. Because the game needs to find the cfg directory in an expected location, we set the "Working Directory" field to "./dist" as shown in Image 8-12. You should also set the "Main Class". The image depicts a default class; make sure yours is set to the MyNewGame.java class.

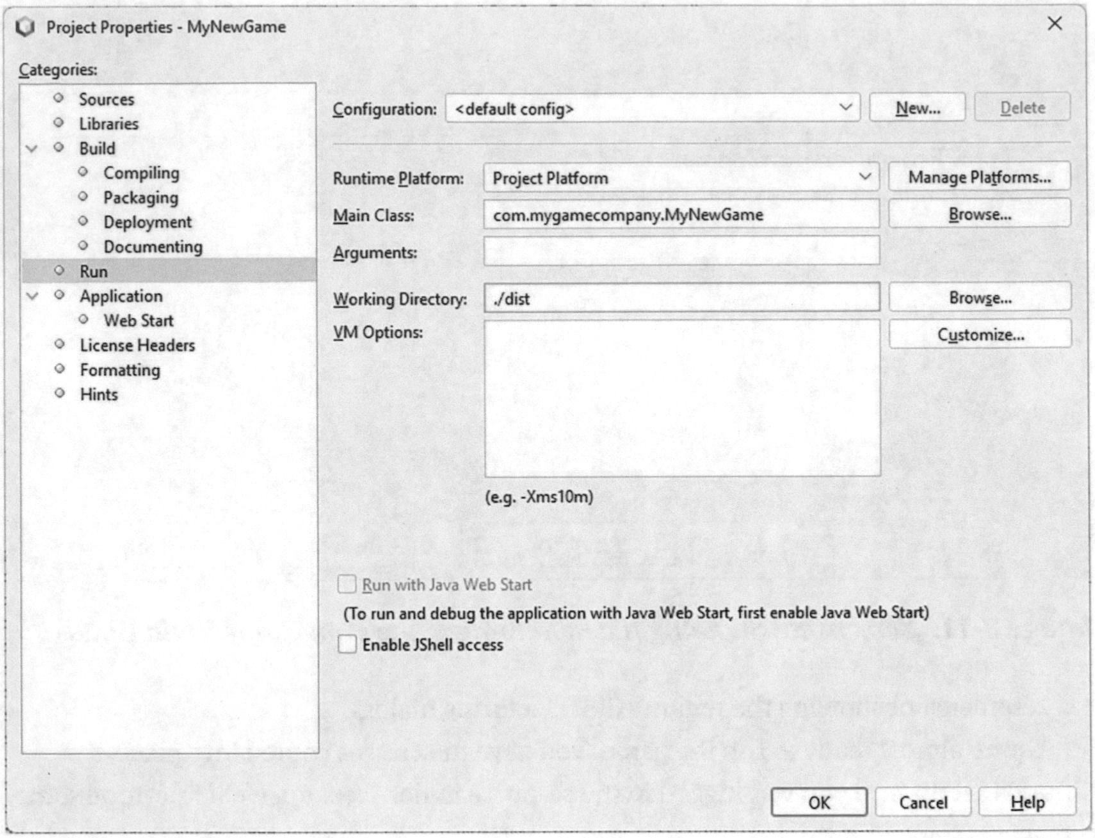

Image 8-12. *Screenshot Showing the New Project's Run Settings*

A screenshot showing the new project's settings configured with working directory and main class.

Finally, we can run the game!

Step 6: Execute the Pong Clone Copy

Make sure the project is freshly built by right-clicking on the project and selecting "Clean and Build" from the context menu. Now run the project by clicking on the PongClone. java file and selecting "Run File" from the context menu.

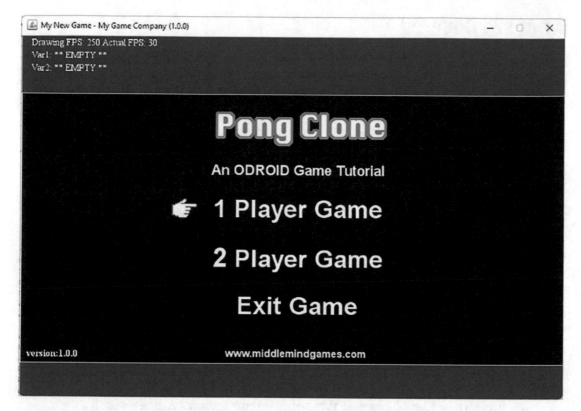

Image 8-13. Screenshot Showing the New Project in Action

A screenshot showing the new game in action. Notice the title with different value than the default Pong Clone game.

Congratulations! You can now create new game projects using the simple Pong Clone game as a starting point. You can clean out the code or alter it as you see fit. Combine this knowledge with your experience modifying games by editing the ScreenGame class and you can start building your own simple games.

Conclusion

That brings us to the conclusion of the chapter and the end of our discussion on Java classes. We got to take a look at a lot of different features of the Java programming language in action and took on a few difficult code challenges. Let's summarize the material we covered in this chapter subsequently.

What We Covered

You made your way through some advanced concepts and a gauntlet of difficult coding challenges. You've earned your stripes. Let's review what we've covered.

- Encapsulation: We discuss the concept of encapsulation in OOP and how to further that concept in certain advanced cases.

- Inheritance: We talked about class inheritance in Java and demonstrated it with a few examples.

- Challenge: Inheritance: You took on a tough challenge using inheritance to add a new weapon, the flame spear, to the Dungeon Trap game.

- Polymorphism: We discussed the concept of polymorphism in Java OOP and demonstrated it at the class and method level.

- Challenge: Polymorphism: You were tasked with modifying the new flame spear weapon further to make it throwable. This took a lot of skill and knowledge. Congratulations for taking it on!

- Importing Class Libraries: Wrapping up our review on classes with a discussion on how to wrap up your code into libraries called JAR files. We concluded the section by discussing how to include JAR files in a project and access the new Java classes in your code using the import statement.

- Video Game Project Structure: One of the more important chapters on applied Java programming, specifically the structure of projects that use the included game engine.

- Challenge: Create a New Game Project: One of the most difficult challenges you've encountered thus far. This one is very specific to the game engine and the project structure. It's ok if you didn't get this one; there are a lot of steps.

We've mastered Java classes and learned how to create our own fresh new copy of the Pong Clone game for use as a new game's starting project. You're ready to start building a game. Look back to the different coding challenges and remember how to add new images to the ScreenGame class and how to control them. You're well on your way to making your next great game!

CHAPTER 9

Debugging Techniques

No matter how hard you try, chances are your first implementation of a software solution is rarely perfect. Most of the time we need to debug our code to figure out what it's doing and, more importantly, what it's doing wrong. In order to be a successful programmer in any language, we need to be able to competently debug a program, so we'll cover a few basic ideas on the subject.

Output Trace

One of the most basic and effective debugging techniques requires no special software, IDE, or libraries. The output trace uses output statements to mark what code is executing and what values certain variables have. Let's motivate the discussion with an example.

Listing 9-1. Example of Using Output Statements to Debug a Program

```
//code
01 public void CheckForMatches(MemoryItem itm) {
02     System.out.println("CheckForMatches: START");
03     if(clickedCards != null) {
04         int len = clickedCards.size();
05         Stack<MemoryItem> tmp = new Stack();
06           System.out.println("CheckForMatches: AAA: " + len);
07
08         for(int i = 0; i < len; i++) {
09             MemoryItem tItm = clickedCards.pop();
10             ProcessMatchCheck(tItm, itm);
11             tmp.push(tItm);
12         }
13
```

223

© Victor G. Brusca 2023
V. G. Brusca, *Introduction to Java Through Game Development*, https://doi.org/10.1007/978-1-4842-8951-8_9

```
14            System.out.println("CheckForMatches: BBB: " + clickFreeze);
15        if(!clickFreeze) {
16            clickedCards.addAll(tmp);
17        }
18
19        System.out.println("CheckForMatches: CCC: " + clickedCards.
          size());
20        }
21    System.out.println("CheckForMatches: STOP");
22 }

//output
01 CheckForMatches: START
02 CheckForMatches: AAA: 1
03 CheckForMatches: BBB: true
04 CheckForMatches: CCC: 2
05 CheckForMatches: STOP
```

An example of using simple standard output statements to trace and debug a
program.

You might remember this snippet of code from the Memory Match game's
coding challenges. In this listing, we're using output statements to trace through the
functionality of the method. Notice that key information like the start and end of the
method call and the size of the clickedCards data structure are tracked. Debugging like
this can help you visualize what happens when a block of code executes. This can greatly
aid in fixing any bugs in your code implementation.

That brings us to the conclusion of the basic debugging technique of output tracing.
In the next section, we'll take a look at the more advanced technique of using the IDE
to debug your programs. Let's take a look at the tools available in the NetBeans IDE for
debugging our Java games!

IDE Debugging Features

Another slightly more advanced approach to debugging your Java programs is to rely
on the tools available in the NetBeans IDE. This has the advantage of being a bit more
advanced, efficient, and powerful at the cost of requiring the IDE to accomplish your

debugging tasks. This is fine, but if you're doing some "on-device" debugging, you won't have the luxury of accessing the IDE's tools. You'll have to fall back to the more basic output trace technique.

Let's take a moment to talk about the debugging features in the NetBeans IDE. We'll keep it high level and focus on the features that are designed to help us find and fix bugs in our code. We won't get into more project-level debugging in this chapter. The debugging button bar in the NetBeans IDE is shown in Image 9-1.

Image 9-1. *An Image Depicting the NetBeans Debugging Bar*

You can find this bar of buttons at the top center of the NetBeans IDE after entering debugging mode, Ctrl+F5. The buttons shown are stop, pause, continue, step over, step over expression, step into, and step out.

To see the debugging button bar, you must be in project debugging mode. Click the debug project button from the top of the IDE window or press Ctrl+F5 on your keyboard to start debugging the current program. In the previous image, you can see the debugging bar before the trace has begun, inactive buttons, and, afterward, active buttons. The NetBeans IDE debugger is meant to work with break points. You can set a break point at any line in your code by clicking near the line numbers, at the edge of the text editor. This will create a red highlight on the selected line to indicate it has been set as a debugging break point.

What is a break point you ask? Well, a break point tells the debugger to stop executing the program at that point in the code so you can look around and see what's happening with different variables at that point in the code. Let's take a look at what a break point looks like in the NetBeans IDE.

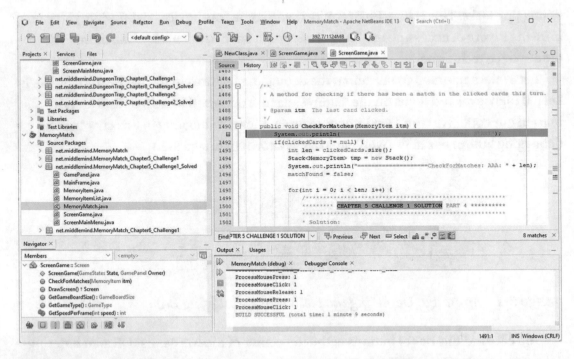

Image 9-2. *An Image Depicting a Break Point in the NetBeans IDE*

A screenshot showing what a break point looks like in the NetBeans IDE.

Let's look at what happens when we start debugging the program after setting a break point in the code before we talk about what the different debugging buttons actually do.

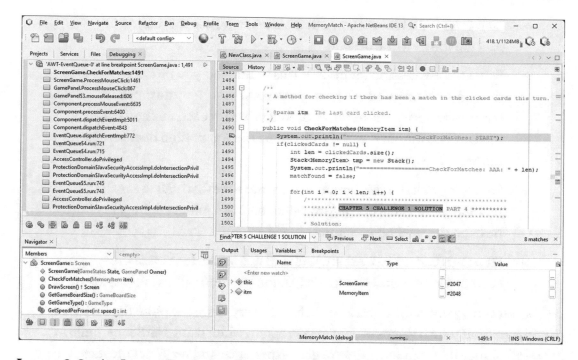

Image 9-3. *An Image Depicting Stopping at a Break Point During Debugging*

An image depicting NetBeans IDE in debugging mode stopping at a break point. Notice that the debugging button bar is now fully active.

When the debugger reaches a break point, in this case, the break point is set in a copy of the Memory Match game from Challenge 1 in Chapter 5. This particular break point is reached when two cards have been clicked on the Memory Match game board. The debugger will detect the break point and stop to await our instructions. We can use all the buttons on the debugging bar to adjust the next executed line of the program.

This feels like a good time to talk about what each button on the debugging button bar does. I'll list them here with a brief description of their use.

- Debug Project (Ctrl+F5): Used to start a project debugging session.

- Finish Debugging Session (Shift+F5): Used to end the project debugging session.

- Pause: A button used to pause the current debug session.

- Continue (F5): Used to continue the debugger. The program will execute until another break point is hit.

- Step Over (F8): When a break point is reached, use this button to execute the next line of code.

- Step Over Expression (Shift+F8): This button lets you proceed through each method call in an expression and view the input parameters as well as resulting output values of each method call. If there are no further method calls, Step Over Expression behaves like the Step Over command.

- Step Into (F7): Use this button to step into a method call to see the method parameters and return values and to continue debugging through the method execution.

- Step Out (Ctrl+F7): Use this command to execute the rest of the current function and it breaks when the function return is completed.

As you can see from the options available, it's very easy to explore the variables, parameters, and return values of your Java program when using NetBeans' built-in debugger. It may take you some time to gain experience and really get the most out of the debugging tools, but that's fine, you were going to be coding anyway. That brings us to the conclusion of this section. In the next section, we'll take a look at exceptions in the Java programming language.

Exceptions

We've had a little bit of exposure to the Exception class, and Java error handling in general, when we talked about Try-Catch statements during our discussion on flow control in the Java programming language. We're going to revisit the topic and talk about a few finer points regarding using exceptions in your Java programs.

Handling Exceptions

Exceptions are generated when a line of Java code is unable to execute properly for some reason. When this happens, an exception is generated with information about the error and a trace of the current execution stack. In order to respond to these errors, we have to use Try-Catch statements in our code.

The Try-Catch statement, as we've seen previously, allows us to attempt to run a piece of code and respond to any errors that might arise when doing so. This can lead to certain implementation decisions that can have broader impacts on your program and deserve some discussion. Let's take a look at some examples of Try-Catch statements. Keep an eye out for some subtle differences in the code, and we'll talk about them next.

Listing 9-2. Example of Try-Catch Statements Catching Different Exceptions

```
//code
01 System.out.println("Exception #1:");
02 try {
03      String s = null;
04      int l = s.length();
05 } catch (Exception e) {
06      e.printStackTrace();
07 }
08
09 System.out.println("Exception #2:");
10 try {
11      String s = null;
12      int l = s.length();
13 } catch (NullPointerException e) {
14      e.printStackTrace();
15 }
16
17 System.out.println("Exception #3:");
18 try {
19      String s = null;
20      int l = s.length();
21      l = Integer.parseInt("not an integer");
22 } catch (NullPointerException | NumberFormatException e) {
23      e.printStackTrace();
24 }
25
26 System.out.println("Exception #4:");
27 try {
```

```
28      String s = null;
29      int l = s.length();
30      l = Integer.parseInt("not an integer");
31 } catch (Exception e) {
32      e.printStackTrace();
33 }

//output
01 Exception #1:
02 java.lang.NullPointerException
03      at net.middlemind.PongClone.NewClass.main(NewClass.java:290)
04
05 Exception #2:
06 java.lang.NullPointerException
07      at net.middlemind.PongClone.NewClass.main(NewClass.java:298)
08
09 Exception #3:
10 java.lang.NullPointerException
11      at net.middlemind.PongClone.NewClass.main(NewClass.java:306)
12
13 Exception #4:
14 java.lang.NullPointerException
15      at net.middlemind.PongClone.NewClass.main(NewClass.java:315)
```

An example demonstrating the use of different Try-Catch statements designed to catch different exceptions.

Looking at exception examples #1 and #2, on lines 1–15, we have two seemingly identical Try-Catch statements. Can you spot the difference between the two? If you thought that the exceptions being caught are different, then you thought right. The first example uses the Exception class; this is the super-class of all other Java exceptions. Catching an exception of this type doesn't give us any information about what went wrong.

The following Try-Catch statement, exception #2, is similar, but it is designed to catch a NumberFormatException, which is a more specific exception class. This version of the Try-Catch statement is more intuitive because you can clearly see what type of error the code is designed to handle. In general, I agree with this approach. Sometimes, however, I go against the grain and implement the more general Try-Catch statement. Why?

Well, there are many cases you'll encounter when writing Java programs and games of different sorts where you really don't care what the error was. All you really care about was that there was an error at all. This is perfectly fine if you don't derive value from using more specific exception classes. Just keep in mind that best practices recommend that we do.

The last two examples in the code snippet, exceptions #3 and #4, present a new version of the Try-Catch statement. One that is able to catch multiple types of exceptions. Direct your attention to line 23; notice that the catch clause of the Try-Catch statement is designed to catch both a `NullPointerException` and a `NumberFormatException`. Juxtapose this with the last exception example where only the super-class, `Exception`, is caught. In this case, we have a lot less information about the code in the Try-Catch look. We don't know what exceptions it might throw. Note that the code must be adjusted to throw each type of exception since whichever exception that is encountered first will exit the Try clause.

This comes back to the same point of form vs. function. If knowing the type of exception is beneficial to you and it makes your code more intuitive and reusable, then use that approach. If you are simply concerned with knowing when something failed and not why, then don't use more specific exceptions in your Try-Catch statements. In the next section, we'll talk a little bit about how to define our own exceptions to use in our Java programs.

Defining Exceptions

Exceptions, like everything else in Java, are based on classes. As I've alluded to previously, all exceptions in the Java programming language are subclasses of the `Exception` super-class. As such, you can define your own exceptions to use in your code. Let's take a look at an example.

Listing 9-3. Example of Defining a Custom Exception Class

```
1 public class MyException extends Exception {
2     public MyException(String errorMessage) {
3         super(errorMessage);
4     }
5 }
```

An example demonstrating the creation of a custom exception class.

As you can see from the previous listing, we've used inheritance, a powerful OOP tool in our coding toolbox, to create a new exception class based on the main one. Now that we've designed a custom exception, we can use it in specific places where we see fit. Let's motivate the discussion with another example employing the exception class we just created: MyException.

Listing 9-4. Example of Using a Custom Exception Class

```
//code
1 public void ProcessImage(MmgBmp image) throws MyException {
2     if(image.GetWidth() < 10 || image.GetHeight() < 10) {
3         throw new MyException("Image resource is too small!");
4     }
5 }
```

```
//output
1 net.middlemind.PongClone.MyException: Image resource is too small!
2    at net.middlemind.PongClone.NewClass.main(NewClass.java:302)
```

An example demonstrating the use of a custom exception class.

In the previous listing, we can see the use of the MyException class. In this example, we use the exception in a fictional ProcessImage method. This method takes an MmgBmp, image resource argument, and returns no value. The purpose of this method is to check the passed-in image argument and make sure its dimensions are larger than 10 pixels in width and height. If not, an exception is thrown.

Note that the method declares what exceptions are thrown in the body of the method using the throws keyword in the method declaration. There can be multiple, comma-separated entries here. When we want to throw an exception, we use the throw keyword followed by the instance of the exception class that we want to throw. In this example, we're using our fictional MyException class and providing a descriptive error message. Why is this implementation not ideal?

The reason why it isn't an ideal implementation is because the exception class is not indicative of the error it is designed to represent. This is not as intuitive as say naming our exception class ImageResourceException as opposed to MyException. Again, being intuitive and clear is the better implementation choice. In the next section, we'll briefly look at the information that comes back from a thrown exception, namely, the stack trace.

The Stack Trace

An important aspect of programming in Java is being able to handle unforeseen errors. These will manifest to you as exceptions and crash your program in the worst way when you least expect it. When you get an exception, you usually get a message and stack trace printed to standard error.

Sometimes, the environment you're executing your programs in will not give you access to output streams. You may have to try to capture and indicate errors in the program itself. In this case, it is wise to implement a very high-level catch-all Try-Catch that prevents the program from crashing completely. This will give you a chance to display some information about the error that you can use to address the issue.

In any case, you should have access to exception stack traces most of the time. NetBeans takes care of displaying any output during project execution right to a panel in the IDE. Let's take a look at an example stack trace so we can get a better understanding of the information it provides us and how we can use it to fix bugs.

Listing 9-5. Example of a Simple Exception Stack Trace

```
1 net.middlemind.PongClone.MyException: Image resource is too small!
2     at net.middlemind.PongClone.NewClass.main(NewClass.java:302)
```

An example of a simple stack trace resulting from a Java exception.

This stack trace should be familiar. We saw this earlier in our review of exception handling. We're using it again here because it's so simple. This code that threw an error was in the static main execution method of the project. This means that the stack trace has only one entry in it. The message provided to us by the exception object is as follows:

```
net.middlemind.PongClone.MyException: Image resource is too small!
```

It tells us the exception class and the message associated with the exception. The next entry is the line number and the class method where the exception originated from. Let's take a look.

```
net.middlemind.PongClone.NewClass.main(NewClass.java:302)
```

In the PongClone project, in a class called NewClass – this is my personal test class – in the static main method, there was an error, specifically at line 302. I'll illustrate the "stack" by moving the exception into a new static method, ExceptionTest. Recall that only static class members can be accessed from a static method without an object instance. Now let's run the program and see what the exception stack trace looks like.

```
net.middlemind.PongClone.MyException: Image resource is too small!
at net.middlemind.PongClone.NewClass.ExceptionTest(NewClass.java:302)
at net.middlemind.PongClone.NewClass.main(NewClass.java:339)
```

Take a moment to look over the stack trace and think about what's happening. There is a second line in the trace now because there is a second entry on the execution stack as the exception causing code now resides in the ExceptionTest method. By extension, this tells us that the first line number in the stack trace is the location of the error causing line of code, while the last line number is the location of the first method in the execution stack. That's really all I wanted to go over with regard to the stack trace printout. You should have more confidence now when dealing with a very long null pointer exception stack trace!

Conclusion

That brings us to the conclusion of the chapter on debugging techniques. I hope you learned a thing or two about how to debug your Java programs. Let's take a look at the material we covered in this chapter.

What We Covered

This chapter was a short and sweet one. We still managed to cover a fair amount of important material. Let's take a look at a summary of the chapter's main topics.

- Output Trace Debugging: We detailed a simple approach to debugging a program where we use output statements to outline the execution path of a certain method or block of code.

- IDE Debugging Features: We also took a look at the more advanced NetBeans IDE debugged that supports break points and a number of actions to take regarding execution of code at break points.

- Handling Exceptions: We revisited the Try-Catch statement and talked about some of the philosophies involved with implementing Try-Catch statements in your code.

- Defining Exceptions: We looked at how we can define and use our own exceptions.

- The Stack Trace: A brief overview of a Java exception's stack trace.

This chapter should give you all the tools you need in your coding toolbox to triage even the most difficult Java exceptions. You'll even be able to define your own custom exceptions to use in your programs to capture certain events or conditions and respond by throwing an exception.

CHAPTER 10

Conclusion

Welcome to the concluding chapter of the text! If you've made it this far, then you've completed a fairly detailed review of the Java programming language including taking on a number of coding challenges designed to get you working with slightly more mature projects and code. That's something to be proud of. You've gained a lot of good experience and built up a solid set of tools for your coding toolbox. Let's take a moment to review some of the things we've accomplished together.

Accomplishments

We've covered a lot of ground together in this text. We started at the beginning and learned about the origins of the Java programming language and then moved on to look at variables, data structures, and even object-oriented programming. Let me outline some of the more notable topics we've explored together while learning about Java.

- Chapter 1:

    - Setting Up Your Environment: A quick overview of how to prepare your Java game development environment and NetBeans IDE.

    - Checking Out the Games: We got to take the associated game project for a test drive.

    - Pong Clone: The simplest project, a clone of the classic game Pong.

    - Memory Match: The next most complicated project, a memory card selection game.

    - Dungeon Trap: The most complicated game implementation, battle enemy waves and survive for as long as you can.

© Victor G. Brusca 2023
V. G. Brusca, *Introduction to Java Through Game Development*, https://doi.org/10.1007/978-1-4842-8951-8_10

- Chapter 2:

    - Basic Syntax Rules: A detailed review of the basic syntax rules of the Java programming language.

    - Keywords/Reserved Words: A review of the language's reserved words.

    - The Main Game Loop: An introduction to the concepts associated with the main game loop.

    - Program Structure: A review of the structure of the associated Java game projects.

- Chapter 3:

    - Basic Data Types: A review of the Java language's basic data types.

    - Challenge: Basic Data Types: A coding challenge to test your knowledge of basic data types involving coding changes to a copy of a game project.

    - Advanced Data Types: An introduction to more advanced data types in Java like arrays.

    - Challenge: ArrayLists: A coding challenge to test your knowledge of the advanced data type: the `ArrayList`.

- Chapter 4:

    - Expressions and Operators: A detailed review of the different types of expressions and operators in the Java programming language.

    - Flow Control: A review of the flow control statements available to you like Switch statements, if statements, etc.

    - Challenge: Flow Control: A coding challenge designed to test your knowledge of Java's flow control statements.

    - More on Variables: A deeper look into certain key aspects of Java variables like enumerations and classes.

    - Challenge: Enumerations: A coding challenge to apply your knowledge of enumerations in Java.

- Chapter 5:

  - More on Data Structures: A review of the most common data structures and their use cases.

  - Parameterized Types and Data Structures: We took a moment to discuss the concept of parameterized data structures.

  - Challenge: Stacks: One of the more difficult challenges involving refactoring code to use a Stack instead of a List.

- Chapter 6:

  - For Loops: We reviewed the different types of for loops in Java.

  - While Loops: A review of the while loop construct.

  - Main Game Loop: Our second discussion on the main game loop where we review in detail a few different types of main game loops.

  - Challenge: For-Each Loops: A coding challenge that tasks you with refactoring a for loop into a for-each loop.

- Chapter 7:

  - Classes: We revisited the concept of classes again and in detail as we covered the most important aspects of Java classes.

  - Challenge: The MmgBmp Class: An interesting coding challenge that is designed to get you more experience working with some of the game engine's classes. Specifically, the image class, MmgBmp.

  - Challenge: The ScreenGame Class: A follow-up challenge that ties in user input to control the image configured in the previous challenge.

  - Advanced Class Topics: We took a moment to talk about some more advanced class topics like class member access and static main entry points.

  - Challenge: Dungeon Trap's Static Main: A coding challenge that will help you understand the concept of the static main entry point in Java.

- Chapter 8:

  - Encapsulation: We took a look at a few key concepts of OOP including encapsulation in this chapter.

  - Inheritance: A review of class inheritance in Java.

  - Polymorphism: The last of the advanced OOP topics that we covered in this text; we reviewed the concepts of polymorphism in the Java programming language.

  - Importing Class Libraries: A brief but informative review of how to create and use class libraries.

  - Challenge: Create a New Game Project: A very important coding challenge where you are tasked with creating a new seed project for a game that includes a functioning copy of Pong Clone.

- Chapter 9:

  - Basic Debugging: We quickly reviewed a basic technique for tracing through your Java code to find bugs and trace the execution path.

  - Advanced Debugging: We also took a look at more advanced debugging techniques that use the NetBeans IDE to step through code.

  - Exceptions: A quick review of exceptions in Java explaining how to create and use your own exceptions.

Even just listing the higher-level topics, the most important ones for each chapter we've clearly covered a lot of material. There are very few aspects of the Java programming language that you haven't been exposed to in some way, but there are some. I encourage you to further your exploration of the Java programming language and learn more about advanced topics like referencing, abstract classes, and interfaces.

Acknowledgments

I'd like to take a moment to make some important acknowledgments regarding the creation of this text and the associated game projects. First off, I'd like to mention two people who helped me get this project finished.

Gabriel Szabo: A consummate IT professional who provided an expert technical review of this book.

Katia Pouleva: A fantastic artist who created all of the Memory Match Pro game art and also cleaned up all of the screenshots in this text.

With regard to the associated game projects, I'd like to make the following mentions. I'd like to thank Pipoya for creating some great, low-cost, 2D video game art. You can access Pipoya's free RPG character sprites at the following URL. Be sure to support and check out all of the great work this artist has to offer.

Pipoya's Free RPG Character Sprites 32x32

The next content creator I'd like to thank is O_lobster. I used one of O_lobster's free dungeon tilesets to build the DungeonTrap board. You can access O_lobster's work at the following URL:

Simple Dungeon Crawler 16x16 Pixel Art Asset Pack

I'd like to thank Robinhood76 and Leszek_Szary for the sound effects they shared on freesound.org. The two small sound effects are the only sounds used in the game jams within and can be found at the following URLs:

FreeSound Sound Effect 1

FreeSound Sound Effect 2

I would also like to thank Chasersgaming and Zintoki, both from itch.io, for their artwork that was used in the MmgTestSpace API's game engine demo application. All of the source artwork along with their original download URLs can be found in the "cfg/asset_src" folder found in the game engine's project directory.

With regard to the Memory Match game, I would like to make the following mentions. First off, the cloud convert website for providing a solid service that comes in handy when trying to convert audio resources between formats:

`https://cloudconvert.com/`

Secondly, I would like to thank the creators of the following free resources that were used to create the game:

Food Icons

Memory Match Logo Source Imagery

Game Board Imagery 1

Game Board Imagery 2

Without the talented and gracious work of those listed here, I would not have been able to get the associated game projects created for this text. Among the various acknowledgments, mentions, and links are some solid resources for video game images and audio. Keep an eye out for them!

Where You Go from Here

It's really up to you what direction you will move in after completing this text. Permit me to make a few suggestions.

- Further your exploration of the Java programming language and learn to use some of the remaining, advanced topics that we haven't covered here like interfaces, abstract classes, and object referencing.

- Make changes to the included video game project. You've had a lot of experience working with the associated game projects throughout the text's coding challenges. Take it one step further and start implementing your own new game features in any of them. Have fun with it!

- Build your own video game from the Pong Clone seed project up. You've learned how to create a new seed project for a video game so why not try to create your own game.

- Continue programming in Java and learn more about the classes included in the Java framework of standard classes.

- Make a version of the Memory Match game that uses the secret Memory Match Pro images created by Katia Pouleva. Look around in the MemoryMatch project's folders to find it.

The sky is the limit. Take the coding tools you've learned here and apply them to any other language you know, your next Java program, or even your next great game. If you are serious about learning more about Java game programming, then perhaps you'd like to learn more about the game engine that powers all of the included video game projects; please visit this GitHub repository:

`https://github.com/Apress/introduction-video-game-engine-development`

The text is a detailed review of the game engine code and can provide you with the next step in your game programming journey.

Saying Goodbye

Well, it's time for me to say goodbye. I hope that this book provides you with some amount of knowledge and/or experience working with the Java programming language so that you can start writing your own programs and even games. Wishing you the best of luck in all that you do. Ciao!

Index

A, B

Advanced Programming Interface (API), 38, 39, 241

Arrays
  copy creation, 61
  data representation, 54
  declaration and initialization, 55, 56, 59
  element initialization, 58
  elements, 63, 64
  explicit array instantiation, 60
  get and set access, 60
  independent copy, 62
  initialization, 58
  instantiation, 57, 59, 60
  length attribute, 60, 61
  lists
    ArrayLists, 72, 73
    data structures, 66
    declaration, 67
    delete option, 71
    explicit approach, 70
    get and set elements, 69
    important methods, 69
    initialization, 67, 68, 70
    solution, 73
  multidimensional arrays, 112–116
  problem solving, 54
  reference code, 61
  requirements, 63, 64
  signature method, 63
  solution, 65
  variables, 56, 59

C

Casting/conversion
  data types, 101, 103, 104
  implicit/explicit variable conversion, 105
  object types, 104
  string value, 101–103
  toString method, 104

Classes, 178, 239
  access modifiers, 158, 160, 161, 178
  class design, 179
  configuration file, 183–185
  Dungeon trap's static main, 181–182
  declarations, 159
  default modifier, 163
  definition, 158
  directory structure, 162
  fields, 160–163
  java file, 162
  memory match game, 184, 185
  NetBeans IDE, 180
  package-private, 160
  private/protected access modifier, 161
  public access modifier, 162, 163
  static main entry point, 179–181
  superclass/interfaces, 158
  XML configuration, 183

V. G. Brusca, *Introduction to Java Through Game Development*, https://doi.org/10.1007/978-1-4842-8951-8

Printed in the United States
by Baker & Taylor Publisher Services